CW01376240

GUIDE TO BODY LANGUAGE

GUIDE TO BODY LANGUAGE

Dilys Hartland & Caroline Tosh

CAXTON REFERENCE

© 2001 Caxton Editions

This edition published 2001 by Caxton Publishing Group Ltd,
20 Bloomsbury Street, London, WC1B 3QA.

Design and compilation by The Partnership Publishing Solutions Ltd,
Glasgow, G77 5UN

All rights reserved.
No part of this publication may be reproduced, stored in a retrieval system, or transmitted, in any form or by any means, electronic, mechanical, photocopying, recording or otherwise, without the prior permission of the copyright holder.

Printed and bound in India

Contents

1 Introduction 7

2 Other forms of non-verbal communication 27

3 Why should we understand body language? 35

4 Gestures and gesticulation 49

5 Conscious and unconscious body language 77

6 Personal space 83

7 Men, women and personal space 103

8 Eye contact 107

9 Standing or sitting: the top dog 119

10 Arms and the man (and woman)	127
11 The language of legs	139
12 Head, face and neck language	149
13 The body language of sex	165
14 Posture	183
15 Making body language work for you	191
16 Body language in the workplace	213
In conclusion...	225

Introduction

People are entirely social animals. We have a great need to communicate with one another and to do this, we tend to make use of spoken and written language in order to convey our message. However, this has not always been the case. Many thousands of years ago, man used mainly gestures to communicate. However, as civilisation developed and man was required to use his hands for holding tools and other activities necessary for survival, a verbal form of communication started to develop and language was born. However, non-verbal forms of communication were not eradicated and are as necessary to communication as they were thousands of years ago. We can still communicate an enormous amount of information to other people without even opening our mouths. This form of communication is more concerned with emotions and states-of-mind than with factual information but it can affect our interaction with people on a daily basis.

This book is a brief introduction to a language without words: the language of our own bodies. It's estimated that between 60–80 per cent of our communication with others is non-verbal; that is, we tell other people more about ourselves by what we don't say than by what we do say. The non-verbal communication conveyed by our body language is a fascinating phenomenon. People who have not studied it are unlikely to realise just how much information they exude without even having to open their mouths and how effectively our body language is read by other people, no matter how subtle it is or how little we are aware of it. How many times have you come home from work to have your partner ask you what the matter is. When we are in a bad mood, even if we attempt to feign cheeriness, our bodies give us away. In this case, it may have been our slouched shoulders or a slight frown on our face, but our it is as clear to our partner as if we had come out and complained verbally.

Studies have shown that the human body is capable of producing over 700,000 different movements. This includes every movement we make, such as standing up and walking. However, it has also been shown that many of these movements are discreet signals that we may not even be aware of making. When we nod our head, we usually mean to

Introduction

signal our approval of something. If we point our finger at our ear, we usually mean to tell someone to listen carefully. When we roll our eyes up as far as they will go and tilt our head slightly, this tends to mean that we are annoyed or have had enough of a particular things or person. When we smile or laugh, this tends to mean that we are happy – an example of body language that can be very infectious and is a universal signal for happiness that does not vary from culture to culture. We will consider many more examples of body language in the following chapters as well as considering ways in which becoming more aware of these signals can help us to communicate with other people more successfully.

Some examples of body language can have more than one meaning and this can cause confusion. For example, when we cry, we are usually upset about something and this is how we express our sense of sadness. However, this can also mean the exact opposite – that we are extremely happy. When we cross our arms, this can be seen to mean that we are defensive people or is can simply be that we are a little cold. When we touch our noses, it can suggest that we are self-conscious in some way, or it could simply be that we have an itch that we wish to scratch. If we go about with our coat buttoned up to the collar this can signify that we are stand-offish or unwilling to join in. However, it could be that we are wearing an unsuitable outfit underneath and wish to cover it up. The hitchhiking pose, arm extended with thumb pointed up, can cause great offence in other cultures. These examples of body language that can be read in different ways show just how important it is to look out for more than one signal to confirm your interpretations. If there are several signals that a person has a particular character trait then he probably does possess this trait. However, if he only shows a couple of examples of body language that signify that particular trait then it is more likely that there is another explanation for the body language you have witnessed. It is therefore very important that body language is considered in the context of the situation in which it is displayed. So look for body language in clusters of signals with common meanings. We will look at clusters of body language in greater depth in a later chapter.

We tend to be unconscious of the body language signals that we are continuously sending out to other people but, at the same time, we are usually able to interpret the signals that other people give off, whether we are doing this consciously or unconsciously. Much of our interpretation of the body language of people is down to our powers of intuition rather than being something more tangible such as our sense of smell or taste.

When we wish to become closer to a person, often

Introduction

words are insufficient to express how we feel and we need to use body language to convey our message more directly. Our body language is also instrumental in affecting how our spoken words are interpreted. Body language can serve to detract from or enhance the power of a message. In British culture we are often perceived as being colder than other cultures. This tendency to understate our emotions can increase the need for body language to add intensity or sincerity to the message that we are trying to give out. Often just by maintaining eye contact for slightly longer than usual or by maintaining an upright posture can have the desired effect. At the same time, if we are trying to tell a partner how much they mean to us but as we do we avoid eye contact and fidget uncomfortably, then we are detracting from what we are saying and ruining the romance of the moment.

While in this book we will learn to interpret both our own and other people's body language, in general, body language occurs unconsciously. Yet this body language is conveying more of a message to the outside world than the spoken language that we actually use. Think how carefully we tend to form speech and how we think about what we are gong to say and select the most appropriate language in which to do it. Then consider all the unconscious messages that you are giving out with your body. It is therefore a good idea that we become more conscious and aware of our own body language. The benefits of becoming more aware of our own body language is something that we will look at in chapter three.

We can learn to use our body language for different purposes and also just as importantly we can learn to understand and interpret body language of others. It is important to note that the meaning of body language can vary depending on the context in which it occurs and the culture of the person who is using or interpreting the body language. How we can interpret body language depends on the situation, the culture, the relationship we have with the person as well as the gender of that person. This means that there is not one signal that has the same meaning all over the world so it is important to be wary of gestures and signals that you give out according to where you are and who you are talking to. If you fail to exercise caution when using body language then you could end us causing offence or even getting into trouble. We have already touched upon the idea that body language is closely intertwined with the spoken word as well as the entire pattern of a person's behaviour and psychological makeup. In addition to this, various body language signs can complement each other to make a particular meaning all the more clear or to strengthen or detract from what is being said and the ultimate message that we wish to convey.

Introduction

It is difficult to convey the enormous potential of body language in mere words. In the past, certain political groups have developed special codes made up of types of body language when language has been to dangerous a form of communication.

While verbal communication is highly reliant on sound to convey the intended meaning, the phenomenon of movement is equally as important for non-verbal communication. Each tiny movement that we make, whether it be in our face, with our head, our legs, our feet, combines with the other movements and gestures that we make to refine the signal that we are giving out. Often it is not enough to read one aspect of body language to gauge what a person's state of mind is. We must consider their body language from a cumulative perspective and make our deductions from that. For example displays various attributes of nervous behaviour such as a nervous tic, a sloughed posture and a tendency to stutter then it is probably a fair assumption to interpret the fact that they have their arms crossed in front of their body as a sign of nervousness. However if a person have an open posture and a happy smiling face then their crossed arms are less likely to be a sign of nerves and more likely to be a sign that they are cold.

Gestures or gesticulations which can be defined as combinations of a series of smaller body movements, can be learned and thus can be seen to vary from culture to culture. The fact that gestures such as these are learned just as we learn language can be seen when young children attempt to use gestures but, to the amusement and occasionally the embarrassment of the adults, get one part of it wrong. When we want to express our approval of something, it is common in parts of the western world to form a fist while extending our thumb – otherwise known as a 'thumbs-up' signal. When we do this our facial expression would probably correspond with this positive message in the form of a broad smile. However, there are probably areas in the world in which this gesture has no meaning or is even considered to be an offensive signal. It can be quite amusing as well as embarrassing and even dangerous, when a gesture means one thing in one culture and another thing in another culture. It is therefore important that when we travel abroad we should try and read up on what gestures are used and what gestures are considered offensive. When in doubt, try to use a gesture that is neutral.

A very different form of body language is the learned sign language of deaf people. While this language is reliant on a serious of gestures, some of which may be comprehensive to people that do not know how to sign, this is a learned language that transmits conscious and deliberate messages to other people. The body language that we are looking at is

Introduction

largely unconscious.

We all judge each other by first impressions, even though we think we should not do this (how often have you heard someone say 'Well, I don't really know her, and I know I shouldn't make a snap judgement, but…'). The fact is, that when we look at a complete stranger walking down the street, or when a new person walks in the room, we decide at once whether we like that person or not, whether we would give them a job or not. Our judgement may be subjective, and modified by time: for instance, a nervous or insecure person may give out 'aggressive' body language designed for protection. Once you get to know that person and their guard relaxes, a different person can emerge. Experienced interviewers know that anxiety and tension can inspire an interviewee to display body language that is not indicative of their characteristics and which may change once they relax and become 'themselves' again. It's up to them to take a chance on whether or not they want to employ that person and often the interviewer has to both read and look beyond the body language of the candidate.

With the development of spoken languages (appropriately known in old-fashioned terms as 'tongues') humans developed a subtlety and a sophistication that lifted them beyond the bodily expressions of animals, and nobody would deny that speech is a marvellous and sensitive tool for communication and that to a great extent our societies are built upon it. But we shouldn't forget that other, older and more primal language either – one that can often give us away in spite of ourselves. For words and speech can also be used as a cloak to disguise our real selves and our real feelings.

Take a typical party scene, for example: a group of unrelated people who may or may not know each other, talking to other people, perhaps about themselves and their lives. Their talk may be superficial and it may even be untrue ('I love my job'; 'We had a marvellous holiday there'; 'My son is doing really well at school'.) but we have to take it at face value; afterwards we may analyse that person and say: 'Sarah said she really loved her job, but I got the feeling she didn't'. What gave you the feeling she didn't? More often than not something about that person's demeanour – tone, gaze, way of standing, a movement of the hands – will have given you a strong impression to the contrary. In other words: body language.

To give another example, from the same party. We look at two people sitting together talking on a sofa. Their heads and faces are turned to each other speaking, but we find ourselves thinking they don't much like each other. Why? In many cases, although for purposes of speaking their heads and faces may be

Introduction

turned towards each other, their bodies, legs and feet will be turned away from each other. In body language, this signals a lack of empathy, a desire to be anywhere else but sitting talking to that person.

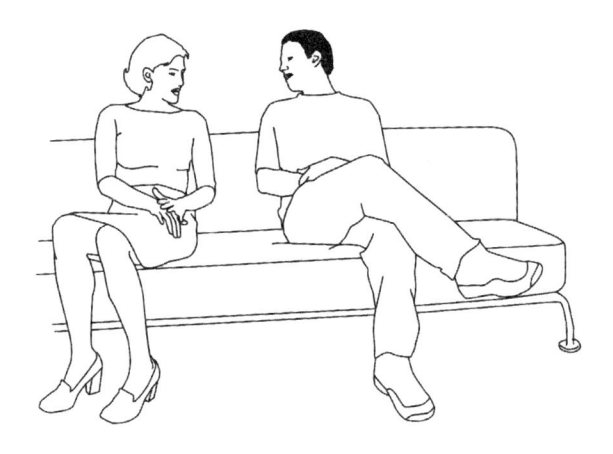

We can consciously control what we say and speak – in fact most situations demand that we do so. In most work situations, for example, we quickly learn to say the 'right thing' – you'd be a fool, after all, if you really told the boss what you thought of his ideas. Politicians spend their lives toeing the party line: the contemporary buzz word is being 'on message'. At work, in society, we are increasingly required to be on message and are judged by what we say.

Our personal lives are seldom free from the need to control our words, either. Very few families or friendships are free of the tensions that arise (often quite necessarily) because we want to keep the peace and not say what we really think about another person's actions or attitudes or just that we don't, really, like them very much. Family Christmases are a prime example of times when members of the same family walk around rather tight-lipped, trying not to express their true feelings in words! (And note the expression: tight-lipped. It's as if the words themselves will force their way out if we don't keep our lips firmly together, preventing their escape.)

In such situations our bodies will almost inevitably give us away: instead of giving a cousin or 'friend' a wholehearted hug and a smacking great kiss, we peck them politely in the vague direction of a cheek. If we sit beside them on the sofa, our bodies may actually turn away from each other, as described above. If person A has to hand something to person B (such a cup of tea), person A unconsciously takes great care not to brush B's hand, or make any kind of physical contact.

As body language is an often involuntary reaction that is interpreted by intuition then it is highly apt that it is a language that we tend to use to express our feelings rather than to voice our opinions. For example, when meeting someone that we do not like

Introduction

very much, politeness forbids us to actually come out and say this to them. However, it is just as difficult to pretend to have warm feelings towards them when the opposite is true. By using our body language, we can maintain acceptable levels of politeness whilst making our feelings absolutely clear. Sending out signals that we dislike someone can be like an intentional statement to tell them of our true feelings, or can be a reaction that we neither help nor disguise. Whatever is left unspoken in order to conform to politeness will be said in no uncertain terms with our bodies. Often this mixed message can meant that the person on the receiving end ends up feeling confused. We are being polite to them and possible even extending an invitation to them but our body language is virtually screaming out how much we dislike them. Even if we do not intend to show them our true feelings, they can often be very difficult to hide. This is another reason that we should try to be more aware of the body language that we give out. If we are aware of the signals we give off when meeting someone that we dislike then we can at least attempt to tone these signals down and thus avoid another person unnecessary hurt and offence. As more attention is given to our body language than is given to our words, then we are undermining our words if we give out a conflicting message with our bodies.

Although body language is essentially non-verbal,

it's an interesting aside just how many words and phrases in the English language reflect what our bodies say. I've used one example – tight-lipped – above, suggesting people who are keeping their mouths clamped shut to avoid saying what they really want to. Here are a few more examples:

She went into it with her eyes open – meaning that someone was totally aware of what she was letting herself in for with a certain commitment. In body language, people tend to clamp their hand over their eyes when there is something they don't want to 'see' (that is, some truth they don't want to face.)

And so I was just left at the airport, kicking my heels – any movement such as tapping the foot, and kicking or drumming the heels suggests boredom, impatience, annoyance, or a combination of all three.

That book was a real eye-opener – as above, open eyes suggest awareness, and when we are told something we don't believe, or find surprising, we tend to open our eyes widely to exaggerate the effect of astonishment.

That was a real kick in the stomach – people often say this while actually holding their stomachs, or touch their stomachs while talking of painful or unpleasant experiences. The stomach is one of the most vulnerable parts of our body, and it is not just pregnant women who frequently touch their stomachs for reassurance or a sense of self-preservation.

Introduction

Babies have no concept of personal space: they are not really sure where they end and someone else begins, and the process of growing up involves learning those boundaries. A happy child tends to be more relaxed about those boundaries, respecting them but happy to cross or fuzz them for cuddles and kisses or the kind of personal contact they have experienced as good. The hurt or damaged child views personal space more jealously, as a fortress to be guarded rather than a joy to be shared. A child who has received a great deal of unconditional affection becomes the adult who does a lot of touching because it's nice to do; the damaged child tends to be suspicious of overt displays of affection.

That's simplifying it grossly, of course, because we can all learn to be more open and spontaneous in our behaviour, and you can be a loving and caring person without necessarily 'touching and feeling' all the time either. Indeed, many warm and affectionate people have a dislike of physical contact with others for all sorts of different reasons.

We have mentioned that body language can vary from country to country and culture to culture. One example of this is the way in which the British have always been traditionally bewildered (if not disgusted) by the way in which Mediterranean or European men who are not homosexual are quite happy to kiss each other on the cheek in public as a greeting and a mark of respect or affection. In some cultures, religious observance determines behaviour to the extent that men and women who are not of the same family simply don't interact with each other socially: it is thus inappropriate to attempt to analyse their body language in the terms we might apply to our own culture.

For various reasons, the British nation emerged from the Victorian era and the early years of the twentieth century with a view that it was best not to show emotion: the 'stiff upper lip' (another phrase connected with body language that has entered our verbal language too) of tradition was a body language all its own, polite but distant. It is interesting to see how things have changed.

Sport is one example. Traditionally, the British sportsman (or woman, of course) treated both success and failure with the same restrained air of 'it was nothing really, just a spot of luck'. With the growth of television and international sporting fixtures, British players and fans were at first appalled to see how continental footballers hugged and kissed each other in joyful exuberance after a goal – were appalled, and then started to do just the same.

Look at family photographs taken before, say, about 1945 and you will see stiff, posed groups of people, perhaps unsmiling even on their wedding days or celebrating the christening of a baby. We

Introduction

cannot say these people were not happy to be married or to christen their baby: they just did not exhibit their behaviour in the same way. Any family photographs taken from the 1960s onwards tend to be much more of a jumble of arms and legs and broad grinning faces.

As in so many other areas of our national life, the Royal Family have been examples for the nation as a whole. Although the stiff formality they exemplified until recently is largely 'blamed' on Queen Victoria, this cannot really be true: Queen Victoria was a passionate and very physical young woman who wrote in her diary that the marriage bed was, as far as she was concerned, the next thing to heaven. However, long years of grief and mourning undoubtedly changed her.

But look at pictures of the royal family before the 1980s, for example, and you see people who are related, and therefore presumably have some feelings for each other, trying very hard not to touch each other. The present Queen went on a world tour in the 1950s and when she returned and was reunited with her young son she patted him on the head as if he'd just come downstairs. A generation later, when Princess Diana had been separated from her young sons for a mere matter of weeks, she raced towards them, arms outstretched, in an unforgettable image of uncontainable and exuberant joy.

None of this is to say that the Queen didn't love her son nor that Princess Diana did; this is not about the quality of their motherhood, but about how they showed it.

Other interpretations (apart from that simply of changing times and fashions) may be that the Queen is said to be very shy, and a woman who hates to show her personal feelings for the camera lens; her late daughter-in-law, on the hand, could be said to be very practised and proficient in manipulating the camera lens and the media in a way she wanted. In the moment that she rushed to embrace her sons no one is doubting for a second that she adored them and was thrilled to see them; but she was also engaged in a bitter struggle for public sympathy against her husband, and knew well that a thousand cameras would whirr in that instant.

The stinging criticism levelled at the royal family in the days following the Princess' death resolved itself at its crudest level (and the whole thing was very crude, because we cannot know, nor should know, how people cope with their own private feelings) to the fact that if they felt grief they did not show it.

We seem to have gone from a society of reserve to a society where every feeling and emotion has to be on public display, and we as 'the general public' read the body language of the famous and powerful

Introduction

through the pages of newspapers and magazines.

The media have become astute interpreters of body language on every level. To return to the royal family as an example, there was a period of some years when Buckingham Palace averred that the Prince and Princess of Wales were ideally happily married, and that the media were just cooking up unsavoury stories. In their defence, the media carried photographs in which the couple's body language spoke volumes of their discomfort and even downright unhappiness in each other's company: most famously, the incident after a polo match when the Princess presented her husband with a prize. It was customary in such circumstances for the couple to kiss each other, but when the moment for the kiss came, they both closed their eyes, squirmed and kissed the air between them.

When the leader of a political party – or someone who would like to be – is addressing a gathering, cameras are almost always trained on those senior members of the same party who are listening to the speaker, usually on the same podium. Who would not want to catch a photo of a minister twiddling his or her pencil ('you're talking rubbish and I'm not paying attention to this'), or casting their eyes anywhere but on the speaker ('I totally disassociate myself from everything you say'), or sitting arms crossed in the traditionally aggressive pose ('if I had your job, we wouldn't be in this mess').

CHAPTER 2
Other forms of non-verbal communication

The way in which we communicate is a complex, intertwining combination of speech and gesture and there are many subcategories within these two broad categories of communication. The main body of this book will be concerned with the many different types of body language that there are and what these types of body language signify. However, it is not a good idea to study body language in isolation. At this point, it is worth looking at other forms of communication that are non-verbal – that is, they do not rely on words to convey meaning but are not strictly body language either. The following, while not strictly body language, can be used to enhance the power of body language or to alter its meaning entirely.

Tone and Volume of Voice

One such form of non-verbal communication is tone of voice. Our voice is a very expressive instrument and is with learning how to use properly. It is often said that TS Eliot, considered one of the greatest poets of the last century, murdered his own poems when he read them because his voice was so flat and monotonous. If you feel that you are not being expressive enough when you speak then it may be worth asking a close friend for their opinion. If it is the case that your voice is a little flat then it may be worth investing in elocution lessons. The voice can be a very powerful tool and, like body language, can greatly enhance what we are trying to say. An expressive voice is a great gift and can come in handy in various situations such as when you are trying to convey a message but are too polite to be direct, or when reading a story to a child. A sarcastic tone of voice can completely alter the semantics of what we appear to have said. The volume of your voice is also an important form of communication. It is hard to express true anger without raising the voice no matter what words you use. A whispering voice on the other hand can be used by women to appear sexually provocative to men or can be used to create feelings of secrecy, excitement or suspense.

Other forms of non-verbal communication

Intonation in the Voice

Just as the tone of our voice can convey much meaning in addition to what we actually say, so can the intonation that we use.

For example, the question, "Are you coming out?" reads as a straight invitation from the person who is speaking to the person that they are addressing. However, if we change this slightly by placing intonation one of the words in the question to read: "Are *you* coming out?" This now conveys a sense of surprise or even annoyance on the part of the speaker which suggests that they were not aware that the person they are speaking to was coming out and on finding out that they are, are less than happy about it. Combining this with a curled lip would give no doubt as to the contempt that the person is trying to convey. Again, if we change the intonation yet again to emphasise another word in the sentence so that it reads: "*Are* you coming out?" This time, the question seems to suggest that the speaker is a little impatient to know if the person that they are addressing is coming out or not and has possibly changed their mind more than once.

Thus, a minor tool such as intonation can radically alter the meaning of am entire sentence.

Dress Sense

A further mode of non-verbal communication is dress sense. The clothes that you chose to wear can give off all kinds of messages about your identity and how you perceive yourself. We are often reminded not to judge a book by its cover, but sometimes we have to go on what little information is available to us about a person to glean some sort of impression of what they are actually like. Furthermore, we tend to pick clothes that are to our taste and in an indirect way this can reflect our character.

It is a common conception that wearing bright, clashing clothes can make you look fun and confident. However, choosing to wear something of this nature can backfire. Those of a more moderate personality could end up trying to avoid you as they assume correctly or not that you are likely to be brash and overbearing. Likewise, if you have brightly dyed hair, various body piercings and safety pins through your clothes then people may assume that you have a rebellious nature and that if your tastes in clothes are alternative, then your taste in lifestyle may also be alternative, and this may extend to taking drugs or other illegal activities. Of course, it is up to ourselves what we wear. But it is important to remember that people can be very prejudiced when it comes to forming opinions on the basis of a person's

Other forms of non-verbal communication

appearance. If you are worried about the impression that your external appearance may be giving off then it is a good idea to ask a close friend what they think.

Punctuation

A further factor which enhances attempts to communicate but is not to so with spoken words is the way in which we pepper our conversation with hesitations, pauses and non-verbal sounds. For example, if we have not finished speaking but need a second to think about what it is we are trying to say, then it is common for us to make an "mmm" sounds . This buys us some time as well as indicating to our audience that we have not finished speaking yet and they should not interrupt. We can build up a sense of drama by punctuating our speech with pauses and hesitations any by changing the pace of our speech. If you witness a soliloquy as performed by any good actor then you will notice the way in which she punctuates her speech by using hesitation and change of pace. Excessive hesitation can also be a sign that we are distracted and have lost our chain of thought. A complete lack of hesitation, on the other hand, gives the impression that someone is nervous and cannot wait to finish talking. This is a common problem for those who are inexperienced in public speaking.

Other forms of non-verbal communication

Conveying Emotions in a Voice

A further form of non-verbal communication is the human capacity to convey emotion through the voice. Thus we can again completely alter the meaning of a sentence.

A wife saying to her husband that she does not mind if he goes to the pub with his friends instead of having a quiet night in with her will not be taken at face value if her voice strained and loaded with contempt.

This example is one where a person is aware that they are conveying emotion and that what they say is at odds with the way that they say it. But sometimes our voice can give us away and let us down. Consider for example, they way our voice will tremble if we are nervous and upset. If we were trying a union leader trying to give a pep talk to disgruntled workers, it would probably lose some of its edge if our voice trembled as we spoke. Other oral but non-verbal ways in which the body reveals that we are nervous is that we are seen to clear our throat at shorter intervals when we are nervous. These methods of altering our voice and appearance combine with our body language to express the wide range of emotions that we, as human beings, possess.

Chapter 3
Why should we understand body language?

The way in which we are perceived by others is only determined by what we say to a minor degree and the impression that we give is decided mainly by the body language that we use. To give off a favourable impression at, for example, an important meeting, it is of much importance that we are aware of the effect our body language can have and so a certain degree can exert some control over our body language. The person that we are speaking to who is receiving the body language signals that we are transmitting should be gleaning an overall impression of us that she may find difficult to explain. This is because she may not be aware of what it was about us that she responded to or, alternatively, something that made her feel at ease. She just knows that there was something about us that she liked or disliked. Most of us have uttered one of the following statements at some point in our lives: "There is something about him that I just don't trust but I can't figure out exactly what it is. Or, "I really liked that girl – she seemed really decent." Or, "I felt I really hit it off with him." Or even, "I'm not entirely sure that she is being honest with us – there is something she is not telling us." These hunches that we sometimes get about other people are down to our intuition. Body language is a mode of communication that requires that we use our intuition to interpret the messages that another person we are speaking to is giving out. It is therefore necessary that we become familiar with our own body language. If we are able to learn our own body language and the signals that they give off we can recognise these signals in others as well as ourselves.

As with any language, body language is a valuable tool of communication. If you were going to live and work in France for a period of years, you would learn French so that you could feel at home; so that you could find your way about, and have a measure of control in situations; so that you could express your own needs and feelings, and respond to others who expressed theirs. Body language is exactly the same, except that it's a language you have spoken since the day you were born. You don't need to learn it, but you do need to learn how to interpret it and use it if you need to.

It is important to remember that while humans

Why should we understand body language?

have evolved to the extent that they are capable of abstract reasoning and forming complex relationships, they are still driven by biological urges much of the time. Like any other living creature, we are dominated by biological rules that control our actions, reactions, body language and gestures. What makes body language such an interesting subject to study is that we, as human beings, are little aware of the postures, movements and gestures that can tell a conflicting story to the one that our voice may be telling at the very same time. As studies in body language progress and become more readily available to people in all walks of life, and as self-help literature becomes all the more popular, we can start to be more conscious of our body language, eliminating those signals that we feel give off a negative impression whilst using it to improve our social relationships with others. An understanding of body language can improve our chances of success in sales, in business, in family life and in romantic encounters.

In learning your own body language, you can gain a valuable insight into how other people react to you. Effective communication skills are extremely important and necessary if you want to be successful both in your personal and professional life. It has been proven time and time again that non-verbal communication, i.e. all forms of body language, actually has more impact on other people than verbal communication has.

For instance, do people think you are aggressive? Maybe it's something to do with your posture, your facial expressions, whether you cross your arms or put your hands on your hips? In a work situation, do you sit on the desk of a colleague, taking up too much of their personal space and leaning over them in a proprietorial way?

If you want people to continue to think you're aggressive, then carry on doing this, although it's hard to see what useful long-term advantage may be gained. If not, then perhaps it might be a good idea to learn to modify how you stand or walk or look.

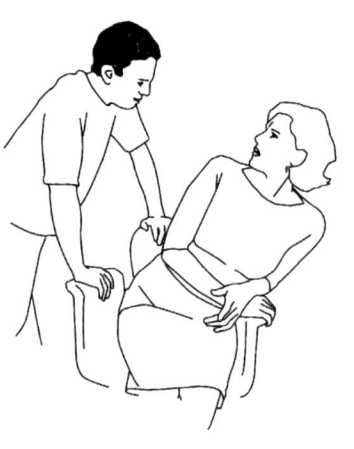

You can also gain valuable insights into your own personality by studying your own body language. To take the above example again, you may not be or feel or want to be an aggressive person, but perhaps something in you needs defending or protecting; perhaps you actually feel deeply insecure, and have

Why should we understand body language?

learned to cover this insecurity with aggressive body language? Such body language may not always be working in your best interests and may even be detrimental.

There are some professions where an awareness of body language is an obvious advantage. An example of such a profession is salesmanship. If you are in any job where you have to sell things or ideas to people, it helps to know how they may be reacting to your sales pitch. Is the person listening to you making good eye contact, suggesting that they are paying you attention, or is their gaze fixed anywhere but on you? Is the person scratching his or her neck, which can suggest doubt? If their bodies are pointed away from you, and especially the feet, it could mean they're longing to get away from you, and you should perhaps back off or cool down if you want the chance of success later on.

If you are the leader of a team, trying to motivate and encourage your team, check their body language for signs that they are indeed alert and open and 'with you'. If someone has their arms tightly folded across their body it could mean they don't agree with the way you're doing things, or that they feel unsure about their ability to do what you do want. This is the moment to say 'Any questions before we go any further?' or 'Does anyone want to query this?' Never, of course, draw attention to someone's body language:

it would be entirely counter-productive to say, for example, 'Jack, you're sitting there in the classic pose of disagreement and withdrawal, so do you mind telling the rest of us why?' This would be seen merely as confrontational and could cause further hostility.

The so-called caring professions of medicine and healthcare are other spheres where a knowledge of body language can help. Doctors are familiar with the phenomenon of a patient 'presenting' with one symptom, but actually more concerned about another, underlying symptom which he is less willing or able to discuss. For example, a woman worried about a lump in her breast which is both embarrassed and frightened to mention to a male doctor, may come to the surgery to complain of sleeplessness, or exhaustion. By examining the patient both in the usual clinical way, but also studying her body language, the doctor may begin to sense that her lack of sleep is not really what she wants to discuss. If the doctor in turn consciously keeps his or her body language open and non-threatening – not sitting behind a desk but perhaps at the corner of the desk, and side by side with the patient, with hands in his lap and legs uncrossed – the patient may relax and feel able to confide what is really worrying her. For more information on how to adapt your body language to the workplace, see chapter 16.

An awareness of body language can also be

Why should we understand body language?

invaluable in our personal lives For example, when it comes to attracting a mate, body language is a huge factor in whether or not we are successful. It has been proven that our first impressions of people are determined by their body language even more than by how physically attractive we find them or by what they actually say.

Many people still fail to realise the paramount importance of body language. When we first meet someone new, we have 10 to 20 seconds to make a favourable first impression. After that, we have roughly five minutes to confirm and establish a positive relationship with that person. Not only do we form our often lasting opinions of other people over such a short period of time, but these impressions are derived far less from what this person happens to say than from their non-verbal communication. This unspoken language is actually said to influence 95% of our insights.

Whilst, when flirting with a prospective partner, body language is essential, in a situation like this, subtlety is the key. It can be easy to overdo the types of body language that are traditionally considered provocative. For example, blatant winking and excessive lip licking can both be considered sexually provocative, but when used in a real-life situation, they can be interpreted as being ridiculous or even threatening by the person on the receiving end. Body language is a far more subjective and subtle mode of communication than mere speech. It's wrought the possibility of misunderstanding as a look in your eye or gesture of your hand can speak volumes.

Try and maintain some sense of moderation and subtlety and you will be more successful and less prone to a breakdown in communication. Becoming more of an expert in body language will ensure that you are sending out the right kind of signals to prospective partners and can also help you avoid attracting more undesirable suitors. There are various examples of body language that can be used to indicate desire for someone. Some popular examples of these forms of body language for attracting a mate are smiling, making eye contact and appearing generally approachable.

Flirting can be considered to derive from patterns of courtship that have undoubtedly been used since the age of primitive man. These signals can range form being consciously given out to being completely unconscious. The greater awareness of these signals we have, the more successful our attempts to flirt will be and the more likely we are to achieve the desired outcome. Those who have carried out researcher into body language generally agree that actual speech is used to convey straight information, while forms of non-verbal communication are more likely to be used to convey attitudes. For example, a woman is often

Why should we understand body language?

said to look at a man with 'come-to-bed-eyes' and can therefore convey a clear message without even having to open her mouth. Either that or this is evidence of wishful thinking and over-interpretation on the part of the man.

In every culture, there are certain words and movements that are very likely to appear together. It is therefore often possible to predict what gestures someone is making by merely listening to their voice and what they say. This also works the other way about as it is often possible to guess what a person is saying simply by witnessing the gestures that accompany their speech. This is especially true during a courtship as both the verbal and non-verbal communication of people who are flirting can be rigidly conventional. This makes it all the easier to study and control to some degree.

In interpreting the body language of others and seeking to control your own, beware of over-simplification and of reading too much into neutral gestures. Also, it is not a good idea to try to use body language to manipulate others. It's almost impossible to 'lie' with our bodies. If, for instance, you hope that a troubled employee will confide in you, it is not enough simply to sit in a comfortable chair opposite them, uncross your legs and unfold your arms, smile and hope they will 'tell all'. If you want your body language to be authentic, you do have to feel some sense of caring and responsibility for the other person; phoney body language is nearly always sensed by other people.

Just as with verbal communication, non-verbal communication can often lead to misunderstandings and crossed wires. We communicate with words and voice tone, as well as all sorts of non-verbal modes communication like gesture, facial expression and posture, all of which can lack precision when communicating and can fail to convey the meaning which we intended. A facial expression, a gesture of the hand, or an inflection of the wrist can mean several things and are often meant to mean something else than what we imagine. Sadly, human beings can often be prone to looking upon the negative side of things and can easily interpret an innocent gesture as a personal slight.

For example, imagine you were giving a presentation to your boss and when you had not been speaking for very long you noticed that she is drumming her fingers on the table or staring out of the window instead of returning your eye contact. Apart from thinking that she was very rude, it would be natural to assume that she was extremely bored by what you are saying. Having interpreted her behaviour in this way, it would then be a common response to start speaking quickly and to finish off what you were saying perhaps cutting the original

Why should we understand body language?

length of the presentation.

However, you may be interpreting this body language in the wrong way which means that your response would be an inappropriate one. In order to avoid misinterpreting the body language of others, a mistake which can cause you to respond in an inappropriate way, it is often a good idea to confront the situation directly. You could for example say to your boss, "You seem a little preoccupied. Would you like to reschedule and listen to the presentation later on at some point." This way you are showing that you have noticed her behaviour and also that you have placed a certain interpretation upon it. This then gives your boss the chance to either confirm that what you thought is correct or more likely to give you an alternative explanation. She may apologise and explain that she is preoccupied with another work issue and that is why she is not giving you full attention. Or it could even be, as I have experienced, that she is trying to make you feel less self conscious during your presentation by looking away and does not mean to appear disinterested. If you had simply assumed that she was bored by what you were saying and had then gone on to cut your presentation short then it may have appeared to your boss that you had not prepared properly. It is therefore often a good idea to ask when clarification when presented with body language that makes you feel uncomfortable in any way.

In summing up, therefore, we should gain an awareness of body language as part of a strategy for better understanding ourselves, other people and that way that we interact in social situations. If you are experiencing difficulties in work or personal situations, it might be worth reflecting on the messages your body language is giving others around you as well as the messages that you feel you are receiving from others.

Lastly, never attempt to use body language for the manipulation or exploitation of others. Somehow, the truth will always out. Our eyes, for instance, seldom deceive others (think of the politicians or public people who can 'do' broad grins, but whose eyes remain cold and unsmiling). You may think that you are coming across as being a very warm, open and confiding person to another person, but body language is almost always a cluster of behaviours.

This means that while gestures (see below) typically involve only one or two body parts, body language itself tends to involve the whole body: you cannot reveal nervousness or anxiety with your feet alone. Generally your whole body (shoulders, arms, eyes, head) will also reflect your inner state of mind. Once you are aware that your body may be revealing tensions or negative attitudes you would rather not have, there is only one solution: address those

Why should we understand body language?

tensions and that negativity at source, and your body won't have to show them any more.

Chapter 4
Gestures and gesticulation

Gestures are the vocabulary of body language: when we speak with our bodies, we use gestures of hand, eye, face, arms and legs. Gesticulation is to body language what nouns and verbs are to spoken language: just as knowing a list of French words doesn't mean you can have a fluent conversation in French – though it's a start – understanding the meaning of gestures is not the key to body language, but it is the basis on which you work.

The extent to which we use gestures of hand or face when interacting with other people varies from person to person; we all know people who seem to wave their arms around a lot while speaking, while others seem to be completely still. Gesturing is also a cultural thing: Mediterranean people seem to use their hands freely to illustrate their words. In contrast, among Asian races, stillness can be considered a physical characteristic.

We may think that we ourselves don't gesture much: in fact we do, but it is so much a part of our being that we are unaware of it, just as we can be unaware of how our facial expressions give us away. If you've have ever seen yourself on a video or a home movie, you may have experienced the shock of seeing yourself as others see you. Until I saw myself on a video that was made during a presentation course I never realised how I used my hands for emphasis: I well remember how horrified I was to see myself waving my arms about like a windmill to emphasise a point!

We are all familiar with some of the simplest gestures: the anglers, for instance, who hold their hands apart to indicate that the fish was 'This big' as if words are not enough alone to convey the size (and, of course, the scale of their accomplishment as fishermen!)

Gestures add warmth and colour to our words: a wooden or bad actor or actress is one who either uses no gestures at all (merely saying 'It's bitterly cold' for instance) or uses them in a false, unconvincing

Gestures and gesticulation

manner. If someone hugs themselves and shivers while saying 'It's bitterly cold' extra life is given to their words.

Another example (at the other extreme of temperature) is the way in which people draw a hand across their brow while saying 'Phew, it's hot!' Such gestures can also have a double meaning, understood without words: if someone jumps on a bus at the last minute and sweeps a hand across their brow to the driver, for instance, we understand their sense of relief and the (metaphorical) sweat they've lost in making it. It's a by-the-skin-of-my-teeth gesture: we understand when somebody makes that gesture having passed an exam or their driving test that they feel they only just succeeded.

Some gestures are used for ironic or humorous effect. An example of this is the way we mock other people's petty or minor woes by playing an imaginary violin. When your colleague is complaining of the amount of work she has to get through before leaving for her annual holiday in some hot and exotic place, you might well mimic the playing of some syrupy sad tune, such as could be heard on the soundtrack of some weepy Hollywood film.

Many gestures are used to accompany words, although they can stand by themselves as purely non-verbal communication. Ask someone a question and they may shrug and raise their palms upwards: whether they say 'I haven't a clue' or 'sorry, I don't know' or not, their meaning is clear.

The point about gestures without words, and a key distinction between gesticulation and body language, is that gestures may be misinterpreted, whereas unconscious body language does not lie. As we have said, gestures may mean different things in different cultures. Using a gesture that is acceptable in your culture does not necessarily mean this will be universally OK. For example, if somebody mouths at me across a crowded room 'What time are you leaving?' and I put up the palm of my hand and push it forward to indicate 'Five' I am unconsciously making a gesture that is very offensive in the Greek culture. Thrusting the right palm forward, with arm raised (as if you were pushing a heavy door closed) is as rude in Greece as making the V-sign is in ours. Its origin, apparently, is that you are throwing the Evil Eye or a curse upon the other person.

Another example of a misinterpreted or misunderstood gesture also relates to Greece. In Britain and the US, raising the eyes while tipping the head slightly backwards is a sign of exasperation: the kind of gesture you might make at the end of an

Gestures and gesticulation

exchange such as this:

> Spouse [to partner]: *Take your cheque book with you. They don't accept credit cards there.*
> Partner: *No, it's OK. I won't need it.*

> [Later on]
> Spouse: *So, did you get it?*
> Partner: *No, they don't take credit cards. I've got to go back with my cheque book.*

The head-tipping gesture is the equivalent of 'I told you so!' or 'I don't believe how stupid you are'. In Greece, however, the gesture means a straightforward 'No'. Thus, repeatedly asking an Athenian 'Is this the bus to Delphi?' and apparently being told 'I don't believe how stupid you are' will not lead to a happy outcome.

The origins of many gestures are historical. An open gesture, revealing open palms, would have been interpreted as 'innocence' or trustworthiness (in other words, I am telling the truth) in those times when such a gesture indicated the lack of a weapon.

The famous 'rude' V-sign gesture (making a V of the index and second fingers, with the palm facing the body) has its origins in the Middle Ages, when English bowmen were the best in Europe, ensuring English victory at a number of battles against the

French. If captured, it was common practice for the enemy to sever those two fingers, thus ensuring the end of that man's career as an archer. Raising those two fingers to an enemy is thus a defiant, 'up-yours' gesture demonstrating angry contempt for the other person.

Another V-gesture (this time, with the palm facing away from the body) was popularised by Winston Churchill during the Second World War. Every time he appeared in public (and in the days before microphones, TV cameras and soundbite politics) and wanted to give a gesture of encouragement, confidence and buoyancy of spirit he made the sign – V for Victory.

Religious practice and older superstitions were the origin of gestures such as crossing fingers for luck, for instance (signifying the crucifixion) or saying 'Cross my heart!' When we make the crossed-fingers gesture, meaning 'I hope everything will be all right' we are harking back to a more religious age when people would more commonly pray for a successful outcome of whatever it was they were engaged in.

Until recently in Christian cultures the Bible was always used for the taking of oaths. Since ancient times, people have emphasised the truth of their words – or, more accurately, guaranteed the truth of their words – by swearing on something widely accepted as sacred and beyond question. In courts of

Gestures and gesticulation

law, defendants in the witness box raised their right hands and placed the left hand on the Bible, while swearing to 'tell the truth, the whole truth and nothing but the truth, so help me God'. These gestures – the raising of the open right hand, to signify openness and 'nothing to hide', the right hand also being the favoured hand, the 'good' hand, the left hand connected to the Word of God – emphasised the absolute solemnity of the act.

When we place our hands on our hearts and say, for instance, 'Cross my heart and hope to die!' this is in echo of those times when the sign of the cross was more widely a symbol of fear and awe.

A gesture from pagan times is the touching of wood for luck. We must add the words too: 'If I pass my driving test, touch wood...' 'If I get into the first eleven, touch wood...'. It's as if we have a deep inner awareness (originating in pagan pre-Christian times, but emphasised by early Christian culture) that it was bad luck to hope too much for something good without first appeasing the gods, who might get jealous of your good fortune, and take revenge. In pre-Christian times, trees – but especially oak and yew – had special significance as symbols of power and magic. Today, when real wood is scarce and most 'wood' surfaces are actually synthetic, many people touch their heads while saying 'touch wood' – a self-deprecating way of indicating our own stupidity.

Pointing the index finger is perhaps the most common gesture of all, although it can have a very hostile, aggressive aspect (hence the phrase 'the police are pointing the finger at him for this crime'). Small children point at what they want, it being the simplest way of expressing themselves without the words they haven't yet acquired. When parents make those first attempts at instilling good manners into their children, it's common to hear the words 'Don't point'. Very small children are allowed to point; once they have a certain amount of vocabulary, it is to be discouraged as rude. Most parents have had the embarrassing-at-the-time-but-funny-in-retrospect experience of being made to blush by a determined small person pointing and saying in a loud voice: 'Why is that man so fat?' or 'Why is that lady wearing such a funny dress?'

When a foreigner with limited or non-existent English stops you in the street asking for directions, pointing a finger in the direction he or she should go is the simplest, and least ambiguous, method of helping. But in normal, everyday interaction, pointing your index finger at a person (although it's OK to point at inanimate objects: 'I'll have that one') is unacceptably aggressive, suggesting an unequal balance of power.

Adults, for instance, feel they can point at children ('Did you do this?') when accusing them of some

Gestures and gesticulation

misdemeanour, or giving them an instruction ('You are to go upstairs now and tidy your bedroom'). Pointing a finger at another person is the mark of an authority figure, a superior: a judge on the bench passing sentence might point at the person found guilty; a senior officer in the armed forces could and probably does point at a junior of inferior rank; an angry customer or client might point at a person they feel has offered a shoddy or inadequate service (the point being that the client or buyer is in 'authority' over the person selling or providing the service). In a more normal business situation, a boss who made a practice of pointing at his or her staff while giving instructions or apportioning blame would quite rightly get a reputation for bullying and intimidating tactics.

In some cultures – Japan, for instance – pointing is always rude, but in Britain, as with so many gestures, it all depends on the context and the circumstances. If some person red-faced with anger points their finger at while shouting and making angry remarks, there is no doubting the hostility or aggression of their intention. It is possible to point at another person in a non-hostile way, although it is polite to raise or lower the index finger ever-so-slightly, so that the finger does not so exactly resemble a gun.

After all, when the National Lottery was launched a few years ago, a pointing finger was chosen as the symbol – although the finger was wreathed in stars and glowing light to accompany the words 'It could be you'. No matter that statistically you are more likely to be kidnapped by aliens or hit by a meteor than you are to win the jackpot, the finger pointing out of the heavens at you from the TV screen or advertising hoardings encouraged the feeling of being singled out as an individual and yes, it could be me.

The same individualising technique was used to great effect in the First World War, when recruitment posters showing Lord Kitchener pointing his finger with his eyes apparently focused on the person looking at the poster. The accompanying slogan 'Your Country Needs You' would have lost a great deal of its impact without that pointing finger, singling out you, yes you, to join up.

Our need to gesture as a way of expressing ourselves is so great that we even gesture when we're talking on the phone to someone; watch people talking on their mobiles as they walk down the street. Very few people can resist using their free arm to circle the air or make shapes expressing the mood of

Gestures and gesticulation

what they're saying.

Gestures come in to fashion and date, as do most other things in life. To make the V for Victory sign while saying 'Peace' will place you in the 1970s just as surely as the 'High Fives' greeting (slapping the raised, open palm of another person) reflects the cool street credibility of young people in the late 1990s and early years of the twenty-first century.

As noted at the beginning of this chapter, gestures are not the be-all and end-all of body language, but the basic building blocks with which we express ourselves. Here's a brief (and by no means complete) summary of body parts, the way we often use them, and what they mean – although remember what was said above about context and circumstances. A popular 'trick' in drama lessons is to ask students to say the word 'hello' in as many ways as possible – confiding, aggressive, enquiring, neutral, cold, happy, drunk and so on. The very same variety applies to gestures.

Gesture: Shaking your head up and down.
Meaning: 'Yes, OK, that's fine'

Gesture: Nodding head from side to side.
Meaning: 'No, that's wrong, I disagree'

Gesture: Patting oneself on the head.
Meaning: 'Clever me!'

Gesture: Scratching one's head
Meaning: Indicates bewilderment, puzzlement

Gesture: Suddenly slapping the top or side of one's own head
Meaning: 'Stupid me! I should have seen that one coming!'

Gesture: Moving the head backwards (tossing the head, like a horse)
Meaning: 1) If the movement is sudden and strong, indicates defiance or aggression: 'Huh! Think you're so hard, right?'

Meaning: 2) A slower, softer movement, particularly if the eyes move to the left or right, can be a beckoning movement: 'Oi, come here'.

Meaning: 3) One slow movement of the head backwards particularly with raised eyes and eyebrows is a gesture of exasperation: think of Victor Meldrew's 'I don't believe it'!

Gesture: Tilting the head
Meaning: Can be used instead of pointing to indicate direction: 'He went that way'.

Gesture: Wiping the brow with the back of the hand
Meaning: 'Phew! It's hot! 'Blimey! That was close!' Indicates either real hot weather or, more usually, metaphorical hot water: a lucky escape

Gesture: Putting hands over eyes (or closing eyes with exaggeration)
Meaning: 'I don't want to see/believe this'

Gestures and gesticulation

Gesture: Widening eyes to exaggerated degree
Meaning: 'You don't say!' 'Wow, is that true?' – disbelief

Gesture: Eyebrows: raising them
Meaning: Shock, disbelief, questioning or mild disapproval

Gesture: Eyebrows: frowning
Meaning: Express irritation or concentration

Gesture: One hand behind the ear, head tilted to the side
Meaning: 'I can't hear you'. (Think of performers on a stage who do this to encourage audience response)

Gesture: Fingers in ears, or hands cupped over ears
Meaning: 'I don't want to hear this'. Again, a protective symbolic gesture, as if we could barricade the ears so that the unwanted words could not enter in.

Gesture: Tapping the side of the nose with one finger
Meaning: 'I know something you don't know!' 'leave it with me, I'll deal with this' – tends to be a wide boy's gesture of smugness in having inside knowledge – think of Del Boy

Gesture: Holding the nose with two fingers
Meaning: 'It stinks!'

Gesture: Wrinkling the nose, especially with frowning
Meaning: Disapproval

Gesture: Raising the nose and head and sniffing the air
Meaning: 'Oooh, that smells good!'

Gesture: Lip-licking – especially if exaggerated
Meaning: 'That smells/looks tasty!' This refers to food, of course, but in sexual terms one person might do it to a friend when describing a male or female they find 'tasty'.

Gesture: Index finger placed upright on lips
Meaning: 'Shhhhh!' Can also mean 'It's a secret – don't tell'

Gesture: Holding the chin
Meaning: 'I'm thinking very hard about this'

Gesture: Shrugging the shoulders
Meaning: 'I don't know' and/or 'I couldn't care less'

Gesture: Hands on hips
Meaning: Defiance, anger, aggression: to a lesser extent it can also mean confidence, being 'in charge' of a situation or it can indicate readiness to enter a situation; in sexual terms, it's a come-on gesture

Gesture: Waving arms above head
Meaning: 1) Moving the arms forward repeatedly is a gesture of aggression e.g. 'get off' or 'keep back'. People on street demonstrations shouting slogans may often raise their arms and shake them forwards, especially with clenched fists
Meaning: 2) As above, depending on context: at football matches, for example, shaking raised arms

Gestures and gesticulation

backwards and forwards with clenched fists is a triumphant gesture when a goal is scored; of course it's partly aggressive too, since if my team has scored, yours hasn't – so up yours

Gesture: Raising arms above head
Meaning: Good old straightforward triumph. At British elections, when the Returning Officer announces the name of the winning candidate (and particularly if there's a thumping good majority), it is a very buttoned-up, anally retentive candidate indeed who does not immediately raise both (or at least one) arm above his or her head in triumph. With palms facing outward, it is also a way of acknowledging the cheers, support or adulation of the crowd.

Gesture: Hands: waving
Meaning: 'hello' or 'goodbye'

Gesture: Hands: clapping
Meaning: The universal gesture of approval, praise or agreement. It can also be used ironically or sarcastically, of course: every public performer dreads the slow handclap, which indicates boredom, disapproval or simply 'get off'

Gesture: Hands: one raised in the air
Meaning: Attention: 'Please may I leave the room?' 'Please may I ask a question?'

Gesture: Hands: Shaking someone else's
Meaning: The gesture of shaking someone's hand when first meeting them and as a greeting dates back

to the time of prehistoric man. Shaking hands first originated as an open-palmed gesture which was a way of showing that you had no concealed weapons and therefore did not pose a threat. This open-palmed gesture changed over the centuries until and many variations of it can be seen today, all of which are intended to show a person that we are not hiding anything from them. For example, opening the palms whilst shrugging the shoulders mean that you have no idea about something and are hiding anything from them. We hold our palm flat against our chest, above the heart, to show that we are telling the truth. The handshake takes the form of placing our palm against the palm of someone else and shaking the other person's hand. This is done in many countries throughout the world as a greeting or on first meeting someone. Length of a handshake varies but it normally last only a few seconds. The participants usually look into each others eyes whilst they shake.

The universal gesture of greeting. In British culture, we tend to shake hands only when we first meet someone and then only in a formal setting: two teenagers introduced at a party, or people introduced to each other in a pub, would not usually shake hands. In many continental cultures, however, you always shake hands with everyone, every time you encounter them – it's a more formal greeting than a kiss, but it is impolite to meet someone and not shake their hand.

It's generally agreed that a handshake should be a

Gestures and gesticulation

cool, firm, downward shake, once only. We tend to judge people by their handshakes: for instance, we recoil from 'sweaty palms' and like handshakes to be neither limp nor over-strong. A limp handshake indicates that a person is low in self-confidence, easily manipulated and weak in character. The person who wrenches your hand up and down repeatedly as if they were pumping up a jack we regard as overbearing, coming on too strong.

If you're handshake is too strong, it could be painful to the other person. Furthermore, a strong handshake may be interpreted as a challenge to the other person and may therefore make a bad impression. It is best to judge how firm a handshake should be by responding to the firmness set by the other person.

Freemasons recognise each other by having a distinctive handshake: a subtle pressure that would only be recognised by a fellow Mason. This is an interesting example of a common, everyday gesture being given a secretive aspect, as a badge of membership.

Gesture: Hand on heart
Meaning: 'I'm telling the truth'. People touch their hearts when they are speaking of something close or important to them: 'My family are the most important thing in my life', accompanied by hand on heart. Another common use for this gesture is 'Don't blame me'. For example: 'It's not my fault, I didn't tell him'. The gesture emphasises the blamelessness of the

speaker. Beware, though, it's also a very common prelude to a complete lie. Look at how often politicians use this gesture. Check the other body language used with this gesture.

Gesture: Fists: clenching and raised
Meaning: Fist clenching is generally a gesture indicating at least extreme tension and at most anger and/or aggression. In the 1960s, it also became a symbol of empowerment. The Black Power salute (seen to such effect in the 1966 Olympics) was the raising of the right fist, often gloved in black, symbolising the struggle of black people to free themselves from oppression and discrimination. As the symbol was associated with aggressive struggle rather than democracy, it was tinged with negative political undertones. The clenched-fist salute has in various forms always been associated with fascism or the extreme right.

Gesture: Lips: kissing
Meaning: The kiss is the gesture capable of the widest variety of interpretation and meaning. The simple act of placing one's lips upon another person (whether on their lips or on another part of their face or body) can range from the infinite tenderness with which a parent kisses their child (often on the head or forehead, in a gesture indicating protection and care) to the vacuous air-kissing of luvvies and other fashionable folk where a loud smacking mwah sound is made several inches to the right of the other person's cheek, usually accompanied by sounds such

Gestures and gesticulation

as 'Darling!' The aim here is not to show affection for the other person but to draw attention to oneself and how utterly chic one is.

After all, Judas Iscariot betrayed Jesus with a kiss.

The type of kiss tends to indicate the degree of affection. When we kiss people we really like, or even love, we get our whole body as close to them as possible, put our face really close to theirs, and usually plant a firm kiss on the lips or as close to the mouth as possible.

In contrast, the kiss we were told to give Auntie Sibyl at Christmas when we were children was the exact opposite: you kept your body as far as possible away from the kissee, kept your lips firmly to yourself, then quickly put your cheek in the general direction of Auntie Sibyl's mouth, withdrawing again as quickly as possible.

The kiss is not only a gesture between people sexually attracted to or involved with each other, of course, but even in such situations there can be a wide variety between, for example, a kiss of warm affection between two long-term lovers very comfortable in each other's presence to the frantic deep-throat tonsil-sucking kisses of hormonal teenagers at a party. (Sexual body language is dealt with in other chapters.)

Traditionally, the British 'didn't do' kissing: it didn't suit the stiff upper lip image (indeed, kissing with a stiff upper lip is one you might like to try at home) and that dignified reserve so cherished by our forebears. A man might occasionally be swept away by uncontrollable lust and plant both lips on his wife's cheek, but that was about it.

True Brits regarded with horror the way in which kissing was regarded in other cultures as a perfectly normal form of greeting; indeed, even Russian politicians, gloomy men in dark suits with menacing eyebrows, pecked each other's cheeks as a form of greeting, like hens pecking corn in a farmyard. In many Mediterranean countries, for instance, this kissing is a standard 3-cheek job: grasp the kissee by the shoulders, and place your lips left–right–left cheek again in rapid succession.

But, as noted in the introduction, the polar ice cap of British reserve is melting, and in recent years even Her Majesty the Queen has been observed to kiss her husband of 50 years not once but twice (on separate occasions, of course) in public.

Gesture: Hands: kissing
Meaning: In the good old days when men really were men, kissing a woman's hand was seen as a courtly, respectful, romantic gesture; alternatively, if you were a British male, hand-kissing was something only done by effeminate continentals. Alas, it does not seem to be done very much now by anybody except in the world of the performing arts. It is also, of course, a sign of respect for a female sovereign or the wife of a male sovereign. Foreign ambassadors to the Court of St James' still come to kiss the Queen's hand when

Gestures and gesticulation

they take up their posts, as a way of showing respect without indicating in any way that they are her subjects.

Gesture: Thumbs: raised
Meaning: Does anyone not recognise this gesture? It can mean anything you like from 'I've won' to 'That's fine' or 'The deal is closed'; but it is always a positive gesture of approval and success.

Gesture: Thumbs: pointing downwards
Meaning: The opposite. In the Coliseum in Rome, at the end of gladiatorial displays when one man was at the mercy of another, the Emperor had the power to grant the vanquished his life. The thumbs-down from the Emperor meant death. It's not so often used as a gesture these days but the words have entered the dictionary: 'I put my proposals forward, but the manager gave them the thumbs down'.

Gesture: Lip chewing
Meaning: When we chew our lips, it is thought that we must be anxious or worried about something and that there is some kind of uncertainty in our lives.

Gesture: Brisk, erect walk
Meaning: This walk demonstrates that we are feeling confident and determined.

Gesture: Sitting with legs crossed, foot kicking slightly
Meaning: This combination of gestures indicates that we are feeling boredom and impatience. For example,

this stance can be adopted by someone who was at a conference where the speaker had been talking for a bit too long. It indicates a desire to get up, stretch the legs and move on.

Gesture: Arms crossed on chest
Meaning: Crossing the arms indicates that we are feeling defensive and are ill at ease in a situation. Perhaps we feel that we are in a vulnerable position and feel the need to protect ourselves by crossing our arms over our bodies.

Gesture: Walking with hands in pockets, shoulders hunched
Meaning: When we assume this position, it is usually because we are feeling dejected in some way. Perhaps we have just suffered some kind of rejection or had a bad day at work.

Gesture: Hand to cheek
Meaning: This gesture indicates that we are thinking about something and trying to make some kind of evaluation.

Gesture: Touching, slightly rubbing nose
Meaning: This gesture can mean many things and is a perfect example of how it is always best to consider the cluster of body language that is on display rather than just focussing on one particular aspect. When we touch our nose it can signify that we are feeling rejected, feeling doubtful about something or that we are lying.

Gestures and gesticulation

Gesture: Rubbing the eye
Meaning: This is a classic sign that we are finding something hard to believe. We are rubbing our eyes because we can't believe that what we are seeing is true and we want to make sure that there is nothing wrong with out vision.

Gesture: Hands clasped behind back
Meaning: This gesture is said to show that we are feeling angry and frustrated for some reason and feel the need to restrain ourselves. It can also signify apprehension.

Gesture: Locked ankles
Meaning: This gesture is also said to signify apprehension. This is said to be more common amongst women than it is amongst men. This is probably due to the fact that is it still somewhat taboo for a woman to sit with her legs apart, while for men it is fairly common to do so. The ankles remain locked together in a position that seems tense and uncomfortable. This is said to be a display of a defensive attitude. People who display this gesture are said to be more withdrawn than average. When speaking to someone who displays this gesture often, it is best to avoid being too overpowering.

Gesture: Head resting in hand, eyes downcast
Meaning: We are likely to adopt this position when feeling bored. It shows that we are lethargic and finding it hard to muster up any enthusiasm for something.

Gesture: Rubbing hands
Meaning: This gesture is thought to indicate a sense of anticipation. This can often be linked to money. For example, if we are about to come into some money we may rub our hands in glee.

Gesture: Sitting with hands clasped behind head, legs crossed
Meaning: This combination of gestures is said to signify confidence and superiority. It is best to avoid to avoid this combination as it can suggest arrogance and cockiness which can often be considered unpleasant character traits.

Gesture: Open palm
Meaning: This is thought to signify sincerity, openness and innocence. We have looked at this to some extent on the section on handshaking. This action gives the sense that the person has nothing to hide Throughout history, the open palm has been associated with truth, honesty, allegiance and even submission. It is still common to find oaths taken with the palm of the hand over the heart. The easiest way of ascertaining whether or not someone is being truthful is to look at what they are doing with their palms while they speak. If someone is being open and honest then they will display some or all of the palm of their hands. This shows that they have nothing to hide and is a facet of body language that is sometimes adopted by a beggar asking for money. However, if someone is being less than honest she will tend to conceal her palms, for example, holding her hands

Gestures and gesticulation

behind her back, placing her hands on her pockets or folding her arms so that her palms are concealed from view. This is a common response when a child is caught doing something that he is not supposed to be doing.

Gesture: Pinching bridge of nose, eyes closed
Meaning: When we are seen to display these gestures, we are said to be making a negative evaluation of something.

Gesture: Tapping or drumming fingers, tapping feet or staring at the person who is speaking
Meaning: These are all commonplace gestures and are though to show that someone is bored something and is running out of patience.

Gesture: Steepling fingers
Meaning: When we steeples our fingers it is said to demote a sense of confidence and authority.

Gesture: Patting/fondling hair
Meaning: In contrast to this, patting the hair is said to be a sign that we are somehow lacking in self-confidence and are insecure, particularly about our appearance.

Gesture: Tilted head
Meaning: This gesture shows that we are interested in what is being said and are paying particular attention.

Gesture: Stroking chin
Meaning: This is a common gesture that we are said to make when we are feeling indecisive and are

weighing up the pros and cons of a situation.

Gesture: Looking down, face turned away
Meaning: This can indicate deception on the part of the speaker who looks down as if they are afraid that if they make eye contact, the other person will detect their lie. If the listener I looking down this is said to indicate disbelief as if they are too embarrassed to make eye contact with someone whom they suspect is lying to them.

Gesture: Biting nails
Meaning: This indicates that a person is nervous or insecure. It is common amongst adolescents and can be a very difficult habit to break.

Gesture: Picking imaginary fluff from clothing
Meaning: When someone disagrees with or feels uncomfortable with the opinion or attitudes that another person is expressing to them but does not feel that they can be seen to challenge them for whatever reason, it is common to exhibit a gesture that can be seen to show disdain for the other person. Perhaps the most common example of this is then someone pretends to pick imaginary fluff from their clothing. This gives the impression that they are not really listening to the other person and the complete avoidance of any eye contact means that the person who is speaking cannot achieve any sense of complicity with them.

Gesture: Touching someone on the arm
Meaning: This is a gesture that shows we like

Gestures and gesticulation

someone and wish to be friends with them. It is commonly used by people who are flirting with each other and want to test the waters before taking things further. It is best to avoid going overboard and touching someone too much though as this can make people uncomfortable and they may start to question your motives.

Gesture: Feet pointing towards the nearest exit, person looking around the room
Meaning: These gestures can be seen to indicate that a person is desperate to leave a room and can think of little else. It may be that he is too hot and is starting to feel claustrophobic or it may be that he is meeting someone and is anxious not to be late. Whatever the reason, his body is screaming out that he wants to leave that instant.

Gesture: Knees are seen to buckle
Meaning: This is a common reaction if we are asked to do something difficult or if we are feeling put upon. It is a conscious and almost theatrical way of saying that we have had enough and if we take on anymore then our knees will buckle. It means that we are feeling under pressure and are looking for a way to ease this pressure.

Gesture: Pulling or tugging at ear
Meaning: This is a common gesture that can be seen to convey a sense of indecision.

Chapter 5
Conscious and unconscious body language

Some body language we are aware of, and do consciously; some body language reflects our unconscious feelings, and we are generally unaware of it. This distinction is not always a clear-cut one: there is often some degree of overlap. Both types of body language may or may not be accompanied by speech or language.

An example of unconscious body language might be, for example, the person who feels insecure or nervous and constantly touches their mouth as they speak. Another indicator of nervousness which is exclusive men is can be found in the Adam's apple. When nervous, a man's Adam's apple can be seen to move up and down. This is caused as the brain's limbic system which can cause involuntary contractions of the muscles connected to the Adam's apple. These muscles can be contracting involuntarily in order to swallow, clear the throat or express a thought which is ultimately left unsaid. Indeed, often people are seen to clear their throats as a sign of discomfort and embarrassment. This is made all the more noticeable by the close proximity of the Adam's apple to the face – the place where the possible audience's gaze will be fixed. The Adam's apple is seen to move when a man swallows and swallowing can often be considered a sign of nervousness, anxiety, stress or embarrassment. For example, an interviewee's Adam's apple could be seen to jump if he is asked a particularly difficult question during an interview.

Conscious body language is often used, for example, in encounters with a sexual subtext. The woman who is strongly attracted to a man may sit in such a way that her breasts are thrust forward, or keep crossing and uncrossing her legs. In part this may be unconscious, but her conscious mind will be telling her that she wants to be noticed.

It's obvious if you run your eye down the list of gestures described in the previous section that the majority of these are conscious pieces of body language: we don't, for example, kiss people without intending to, or being aware of what we're doing. The aspect that may be unconscious is the degree to which we reveal our feelings by body language. When kissing a relative or friend, for instance, for whom are feelings are not particularly warm, we may think that

Conscious and unconscious body language

by giving them a kiss we've shown affection; we may not be aware of the extent to which we're keeping our body away from this person, or avoiding the lips, or refusing to make eye contact, or turning the head away; in short, our body language is negative although the act itself, the kiss, may be positive.

It's true, if sad, that in many sexual relationships one partner will sense that their partner's feelings have changed: not because they do anything different, but because of the way they do it. In other words, a man may still kiss his wife when he comes home from the office, but his body language is saying he doesn't want to do it.

It is also said that women are often superior to men when detecting unconscious body language. This could be because women are more likely to use the hemisphere of the brain which is used for intuitive and emotional thought processes whereas men are more likely to use the side of the brain that deals in cold, logical reasoning. With women it is often easy for them to trust their instincts and go with a gut reaction about a person and their body language. Their intuition should alert them to anything untoward in the body language of other people.

Unconscious body language can reveal a person's point of view as well as reinforcing the ideas and outlook that inspire the body language in the first place. We have already considered the fact that body language is more accurately read of we look at the cluster of different movements a person is making rather than simply focussing on one. Many therapists believe that reading these clusters of body language can not only indicate someone's state of mind but can also reveal and thus be effective in the treatment of pathological thought patterns It is a common practise in modern-day therapy to read the simple kinaesthetic, visual, or auditory cues that a person transmits in order to detect the thought processes that are going on in their inner self.

For example, if a person is suffering from paranoid delusions then she will speak in a certain way, exhibit a certain posture and use gestures which all reflect this paranoia. While she exhibits this cluster of body language, it will reinforce the state of mind that is causing it. In other words, if this person was to assume an open posture and use gestures which indicate a confident carefree nature then her paranoid state of mind would not be reinforced by her body language, others would perceive her differently and would be less likely to confirm her paranoia. Of course this is simplistic, but it serves to illustrate how a person's body language not only reflects but can also be seen to reinforce a particular state of mind, especially a negative one. It is definitely true that if we begin the day determined to remain cheerful and make a concerted effort to exhibit open, cheerful

Conscious and unconscious body language

body language then this is how we will begin to feel. There is therefore much truth to be had in the old adage, "smile and the world smiles with you".

Verbal highlighting

When studying the body language of others, a significant sideline is their verbal highlighting of certain aspects of what they have to say. To give a crude example, when someone (perhaps a salesperson or someone trying to persuade you of something) says 'Look, to tell you the absolute truth...' – listen carefully and watch carefully. Such a phrase may often be accompanied by the old hand-on-heart gesture, which is often used by those defending themselves as they reveal less than the truth. If we are telling the truth, or if we are speaking from the heart, we don't need to say so, and most people in fact don't. Another such weasel phrase is 'Look, I've got to tell you the truth...'. The key word is look: if you do look, you may end up with the feeling that what you are being told is far from the real facts.

Chapter 6
Personal space

In body language, the issue of personal space is crucial. Quite literally, this is the space we have around us and how much or how little of it we need with a variety of people in a variety of situations. It's well known from countless books and television documentaries how important space, or territory, is in the animal kingdom. Cats, we know, are territorial creatures inhabiting well-defined territories: a dominant cat in the neighbourhood may include several gardens other than your own in his territory; if you have a timid or submissive cat, even his own garden may not be his territory, but he may be allowed to be in it by grace of the dominant feline thug.

The merry chirp of the robin or the blackbird on a twig is not, as poets would have it, a joyful praise of the beauties of nature. According to scientists, the little fellow is saying 'This is mine; this is mine; come here and fight me for it if you dare'.

It's also well known that animals suffer when their territory is artificially altered. The lion roaming the African plains is different from the sad creature pacing up and down a cage in a zoo. Scientists have kept rats in cages in conditions of deliberate overcrowding to study the effects of stress upon human beings.

To many, the stress of the modern world is about personal space: how little of it we have. We live too close to our neighbours: often quite literally, so that the neighbour who plays music or TV so loud that it penetrates your walls and your privacy becomes an intolerable burden. Although we're each cocooned in the personal space of our own cars, traffic congestion is stressful because we literally have no room to manoeuvre.

Personal space

The Body Language of Proxemics

One aspect of non-verbal communication and body language that is of particular interest is that of spatial relationships, or proxemics – a term which is derived from the word proximity. The study of proxemics focuses on how people appreciate their personal space and on how they use this space, and numerous scientific studies have researched this issue of personal space. Like many species in the animal kingdom, humans are highly territorial but in day-to-day life we tend to remain unaware of this until someone enters or violates in some way what we consider to be our space. This sense of a personal space the territorial boundaries that we consciously or unconsciously define can be seen to yield an influence over our daily encounters with other people. For most people, it is highly important that we are able to feel in control over what we regard as our own space. To improve our relations with other and to maintain our own personal sense of satisfaction during social interaction, it is important that we are aware of the theory behind proxemics and the significance that this has in our everyday lives. Studies of proxemics have identified four levels or types of space, or zone. Scientists have gone so far as to actually calculate the space in feet and inches we need to maintain from the person that we are interacting with in the context of each social situation. These four zones will be briefly described later in the chapter.

Personal space

The History Of Proxemics

Proxemics is the name given to the study of man's use of personal space and is a term that was coined in 1963 by a researcher names E.T. Hall. He also spoke 'fixed' and 'semi-fixed' feature space. Fixed feature space is a space that is defined by unmoveable boundaries, for example, specific areas in a workplace cordoned off by partition walls. Semi-fixed feature space, on the other hand, is defined by fixed but ultimately movable boundaries such as furniture. Informal space, the third category identified, is space that is neither fixed no semi-fixed and is further defined as a personal zone or 'bubble' that varies from context to context and on how this space is perceived by the individual.

All three of these categories of space can be seen to affect the social interaction of people within these types of space. However, the area that has the greatest effect on humans is the third category of informal space. Human beings see informal space as somehow belonging to them and they feel the need to protect this from invasion by other people. This need to limit the intrusion of others varies according to the context and according to the relationship that is held with the potential intruder. The study of spatial territory for the purpose of communication uses four categories for informal space: the intimate distance for embracing or whispering (6–18 inches), the personal distance for conversing with those we consider good friends (1.5–4 feet), social distance for conversations among people we are merely acquainted with (4–12 feet), and public distance used for speaking in public (12 feet or more).

Behavioural study indicates that individuals perceive the distance that is appropriate for each different type of messages or situation; they also establish the distance that they feel is a comfortable one for personal interaction and non-verbally define this as their personal space. Research supports the hypothesis that the violation of this personal space can have serious adverse effects on communication to the extent of impeding it altogether. Thus, if an individual is to be mutually satisfied in a communication encounter, his/her personal space must be first of all correctly perceived and then respected. Should an intruder invade this personal space while also trespassing within territorial boundaries he placed himself in double jeopardy and must compensate for the other's increased anxiety.

Here in greater detail are the four categories of informal space that we have mentioned above:

1 Public zone – this is where we need the most physical space or distance between ourselves and others, and would typically be seen, for instance, if one person were addressing a group of others. A

Personal space

manager addressing his entire staff, for instance, would feel more comfortable at a greater distance from the people he or she was addressing than if he was talking to one or two people. In order to imagine what would be comfortable for you, imagine you had to give a speech to an audience of 150 people: where would you want the front row of the audience to be? Scientists calculate that in most people this distance would be over 12 feet.

2 Social zone – this is the distance at which we feel comfortable standing or sitting from people whom we don't know and are unlikely to. Examples would be people we employ to do jobs for us (electricians or decorators, for instance). It's a distance we like to keep from total strangers – for example, waiting for a train on a platform, or standing in a queue. Another reason why public transport, or getting into public lifts, can cause anxiety and stress is that we are obliged to stand much closer to strangers than is comfortable for us. We can rationalise this by understanding that it is only for a short period of time and that the situation demands it, and acknowledging that we do, however, feel uncomfortable. The social zone has been calculated as being between 4 and 12 feet.

3 Personal zone – this is the amount of space with which we feel comfortable when with good friends that we feel at ease with without being entirely intimate. This is reckoned to extend from one and half feet up to 4 feet.

4 Intimate zone – obviously, this involves the least amount of space and we are comfortable to have such a little amount of personal space only when with those who are (literally and metaphorically) closest to us: family, very close friends and partners. We are at our most vulnerable in this area, which is why it is so precious to us. This is calculated as being from 6 inches to 3 feet.

A sub-zone has been described within this category, known as the close intimate zone: this is reserved only for chosen sexual partners. Quite obviously, sexual contact with another person involves surrendering almost completely our personal space, albeit temporarily; because personal space is the 'bubble wrap' we need in order to feel safe and confident, its violation is truly an outrage. A person who has bad or negative experiences in the public zone may retreat into the 'safety' of the social zone, and then the personal zone, and finally the intimate zone. The smaller the personal space, the greater the damage and the trauma when it is breached, which is why rape – which violates the close intimate zone – is such a hideous crime.

Obviously the amount of space dictated by these categories can vary. A naturally shy person standing up to make a speech in public because they believe

Personal space

passionately in the cause involved is going to experience the 'public zone' and the extent of it differently from a born performer and extrovert who craves adulation. Someone brought up in a large, physically uninhibited family is going to have different personal-space needs from someone from a more reserved background.

Proxemics And Territory In The Workplace

As most of us are spending increasing amounts of time at work, it is particularly interesting to consider body language in the context of the workplace. We have already looked at how our gestures reflect our inner state of mind and what message this can be giving out at work and in our personal lives. It is also interesting to look at the concepts of space and territory in the workplace to see how we adhere to these concepts, whether consciously or subconsciously, and how they affect our communication with others.

While the study of proxemics concentrates mainly on the sense of space that people perceive to be surrounding them, when studying body language, it is also interesting to look at how individuals attempt to mark what they feel to be as their territory. Territorial claims are different to the categories of space that are studied in Proxemics. For example, the informal space that we are only happy for people we are intimate with to enter is defined by its close proximity to us. In other words, our presence is necessary to define this space. Territory, on the other hand, does not rely on our immediate presence for their existence. Territory is a stationary phenomenon that can also be seen to exist in our absence.

Whilst territory and the categories of space

Personal space

defined in proxemics can be seen as two distinct entities sometimes the two can be see to impinge on one another. Semi-fixed feature space such as our desk of our particular corner of the office is often a part of what we perceive to be our territory. We feel safe and secure at our own desk surrounded by personal knick-knacks such as photographs and personal organisers. This is why it can be very unsettling when for some reason our office is rearranged or because of a limit on space and equipment we are forced to 'hot desk' and share space with others. Even when forced to share desks and equipment, we still manage to stake out our own territory to some degree and defend this from invasion by outsiders. For example, have you ever noticed that in an evening class or club you have joined, people tend to go back to the same seats that they sat at on the first night? If, for some reason, someone suddenly chooses a different seat to sit in, this can force others to do the same and cause much irritation and even confusion. Someone taking the chair that you have become accustomed to sitting in can be seen somehow as a challenge to you. Humans quickly mark our territory, whatever the context, and are quick to defend that territory by subtle and not so subtle means.

It is also interesting to consider both the territory and personal space of our colleagues and how we perceive these. For example, consider if you would feel comfortable approaching a colleague at work by stepping in behind their desk. Their desk is an example of a semi-fixed boundary. Although moveable and non-permanent, it can nevertheless be considered as a boundary that exists to protect your colleagues sense of space from the greater area of the office. A desk is a key factor in establishing spatial boundaries and therefore affects communication between colleagues, too. The use of a desk in such a way is increasing due to the current popularity of open plan offices. I think it's true to say that most of us would not feel comfortable in stepping round the desk of our boss. However, if it is someone that we are friendly with and even socialise outside work with then we would probably feel more comfortable in doing so.

The open plan style offices with 'booths' which allocate the space allowed for each individual that are becoming increasingly popular with big companies do not allow much room for rearranging the furniture to suit personal preference – other than minimal adjustment to chair and desk height to meet health and safety requirements that is. As space is such a premium, there is often no room to bring in an extra chair for visiting colleagues. Being allowed as extra chair can be considered a status symbol. It can be interpreted that their job is so important that they

Personal space

require the physical room to be able to pass on their expert knowledge to other employees.

The arrangement of an individual's desk and chair speaks volumes about their perception of their own importance and perhaps more importantly their status in the company. To ascertain these factors it is necessary to consider where the chair is placed, and in what relation to the desk. These pieces of furniture can be laid out in several ways. For example, if the worker is seated at the back of the office, and is looking out at the other workers in the office then we can deduce that they are probably a manager or some other promoted position. This is because they are separate from the rest of the office and are thus protected from being taken by surprise. They can observe what is going on in the rest of the office and keep an eye on the productivity of the other staff.

If an individual is seated so that their back faces the door then we can ascertain that they are probably in a junior position. This seating arrangement leaves them vulnerable as their back is exposed and they cannot easily anticipate an intruder on their patch. The close proximity to the door can also be interpreted as they are new to the company and their position is not so stable. This is in direct contrast to the manager who sitting furthest from the door and therefore furthest into the body of the office appears to be ensconced in the company and probably feels more secure in his or her position than the office junior does.

Such physical boundaries as desks and chairs are not the only method by which we define our sense of personal space. People just seem to be aware of their own space and that of other people and can be amazingly sensitive when it comes to respecting the space and privacy of other people. When we are forced into sharing some kind of intimacy with a stranger, we can be made to feel very uncomfortable. For example, many of us have accidentally overheard a telephone conversation that wasn't meant for our ears because the person on the phone was unaware of our presence nearby. The most common reaction of the unwitting eavesdropper in this case would be to leave the room so that he can no longer overhear or clear his throat loudly to alert the person on the phone to his presence, thus giving her the opportunity to censor her conversation.

Conserving our Personal Space

In modern society, we have a tendency to discourage any kind of contact except with our friends, family and spouses – people that we know well and trust. When squashed up like sardines on an overcrowded bus or train, we automatically seem to try and make ourselves smaller, allowing as little contact as possible with other people. While the degree to which we are affected by this varies from nationality to nationality, it is a general human trait that we wish to preserve our sense of personal space.

While we feel the need to preserve our sense of personal space, there are times when we wish to feel a sense of communion and enjoy feeling a part of a bigger crowd, for example, at a party or a rock concert. Furthermore, in situations like these we are happy to relax the distance that we usually keep from other people, as if sharing the experience of hearing a band play means that we become at one with other people. It need not be an uplifting event such as a concert that leads us to transcend our normal desire for preserving our personal space. An event as prosaic and dull as being in a queue at the bank can lead us to have to give up our preservation of distance from other people.

As two people become either physically closer or further away from one another, it automatically changes the basis of their relationship. Drawing closer to someone can signal many things. It can show that one or both people wish to become more physically intimate, or on a more negative note, it can show that one person wishes to intimidate the other by deliberately invading his personal space. People who are employed to interrogate witnesses whether it be in the police or in a court of law, use the distance that they stand from the suspect as a weapon. A suspect is far more likely to be intimidated and to confess if she feels that her space is being invaded and this technique can break down the defences of even the most determined witness. The theory behind this form of interrogation is that by invading the suspect's personal space and allowing them nowhere to retreat to, it follows that the subject will become malleable and less likely to resist the will of the interrogator. This explains why war zones and other areas where human rights are found to be lacking, interrogators often use sexual assault – the ultimate invasion of personal space - as a way of prying out confessions, whether these are true confessions or not.

A verbal message can be greatly affected by the distance at which it is spoken and many types of conversation will have a corresponding appropriate distance between the participants of the conversation. The distance that is required to be kept between participants in conversations is so predictable that if

Personal space

we were given the contents of the conversation, then we would probably we able to guess the distance maintained between the participants. For example, if you were speaking to an employee about their recurring tardiness, then you would not shout this across the office in hearing distance of other people as this would be entirely inappropriate. It is more likely that you would take them aside and stand closely to them as the nature of the conversation is forcing you into an intimacy with them even if only for the duration of that one conversation.

The distance that we maintain between ourselves and others is not only apparent in the workplace but also in the home., both in the layout of rooms and furniture and in they way we interact within the home. Just as we maintain a variety of distances from other people depending on how close we are to them, we also have different spaces within the home in which we interact with different people.

For example, while it is becoming increasingly fashionable to have a large living space in the form of an open plan house and the boundaries of different rooms are being blurred, most people do still consider their bedrooms to be areas and they would be unlikely to host a social gathering in the bedroom. In most homes we limit public access to rooms such as the living room and dining room.

The layout of the furniture is also designed to

allow people to interact in a particular way. In this day and age when the popularity of television and the almost limitless access to cable and digital channels is said to be killing the art of conversation, it is interesting to note that in the majority of living rooms, the chairs can be seen to focus around the television set. In arranging the chairs like this instead of having them face one another, we are limiting the possibility of communication between people.

The theory of proxemics is perhaps easier to understand if applied to a easily imagined real-life situation. For example, imagine two girls sharing a tiny, cramped flat while at university: Joanne is the second of four children, and until going to university had always shared a bedroom with her older sister. The sisters all shared one another's clothes and make-up, and Joanne was quite used to helping herself to her mother's Tampax in the bathroom or using her make-up. Moreover, the family had no shyness about their own bodies, and parents and children wandered around the house in various stages of undress, quite comfortable with this. Unfortunately her flatmate, Marion, was the exact opposite: an only child, she had never shared a bedroom with anyone, never seen her parents naked, and was taught from an early age to lock the door when having a bath and keep her own possessions in her own room. For the first few months of flat sharing, the relationship between the

Personal space

two girls was traumatic. Marion raged at finding that Joanne, needing a Tampax and not having any, had gone into her room, opened her drawer and taken one; there was no lock on the bathroom door, and Marion was utterly mortified one day when she was in the bath and Joanne came bounding in to clean her teeth. Joanne found Marion cold, hostile and pernickety; Marion just felt invaded. Fortunately, before the situation deteriorated beyond repair, both girls were able to talk about their feelings and agree some ground rules which satisfied them both. As the friendship grew, Marion was able to relax and extend the personal boundaries within which she felt at ease, while Joanne learned that the wider world has different rules from family life, and that other people's personal space may have different dimensions from your own.

We've already shown that there are public situations (such as being on the Tube or a crowded bus) where our personal space is invaded to an extent that can be stressful. That's why we seem to have developed a set of unspoken, unwritten rules for such situations that help us cope. In essence, the rule is to avoid eye contact with others and take up as little space as possible. Eye contact is hostile, or threatening; if you accidentally do make eye contact with the person strap-hanging next to you, this unspoken etiquette demands you look away: this is to minimise the threatening potential of this situation. Only by staring straight ahead, or at our feet, and generally pretending that the other people in your carriage or lift simply aren't there can we cope by means of this unspoken etiquette with a situation alien and unnatural for us.

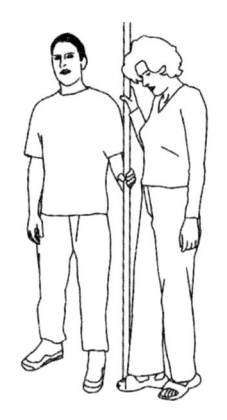

Chapter 7
Men, women and personal space

Studies have been done comparing the way in which men and women seem to occupy personal space, particularly in the social and personal zones.

Men, it seems, are in general more confident at filling their own space and encroaching that of other people. This would seem to link the issue of space (and, of course, body language) with that of personal power. The more powerful you are, or think you are, the more space you take up and the more 'open' your body language.

To give one example: in Western society, women tend to sit with their legs together: the ankles may be crossed, or one knee may be crossed over another, or women sit simply with the knees touching and the legs kept together. On one level, this is merely practical and the dictate of fashion: throughout the twentieth century women's skirts became shorter and shorter, and until trousers or jeans became widely acceptable female clothing, then you kept your legs together to avoid the whole world seeing your underwear.

But keeping legs together may also be interpreted, in terms of body language, as a protective, or defensive, gesture. If you accept that until recently women have been second-class citizens, then the less physical space they occupied the better. Historically, women in our society had to be quiet, tranquil, silent, compliant: in short, invisible. A woman crossing her legs is minimising the amount of space she need occupy: she is also 'covering' her sexual organs, since they are literally private parts and must be kept from view.

Men, on the other hand, tend to sit with their legs apart, not only drawing attention to the crotch and the fact that it is there, but spreading themselves over more space than their bodies occupy: if you sit with your legs apart you are making yourself wider and (if you're sitting next to someone on a train or in a cinema, for instance) actually taking up that person's space.

In what may be a sweeping generalisation, I have observed that when a man and a woman (who are strangers to each other) sit next to each other on a train, the woman tries to be very careful to occupy as little space as possible, often by crossing her arms or keeping her hands in her lap, legs together or knees crossed, while the man next to her (who may also have his arms folded but for a different reason: see below) will be quite comfortable with the fact that his legs are wide apart and he is in fact encroaching on the woman's 'space'.

To give another example. I was for many years a keen swimmer and a regular at our local pool. There are exceptions to every rule, of course, but I noticed far too often for it be coincidence that while women tended to favour breast stroke (a stroke where you look ahead and see what's coming), and swam round other people, men (and especially younger ones) favoured crawl or backstroke – noisier, splashier strokes where you cannot actually see the water ahead of you while doing them. The message seemed to be that they didn't need to look where they were going –

it was up to everyone else to get out of their way.

CHAPTER 8
Eye contact

The most expressive aspect of non-verbal communication is the way that we can communicate with our facial expressions. These are the most observed and obvious of all body language signals. We have a tendency to focus on the face more than any other body part because that is where the eyes are located. Facial expressions are easy to read and tend to be almost universal in their meanings. The meaning of a smile for instance is the same throughout the world and even in parts of the animal kingdom. Thus much emotion can be conveyed in a face and this is done primarily through the eyes. For example, if we say that someone gave us a dirty look or made eyes at us, then it becomes instantly clear what we mean by this.

Poets say the eyes are the mirror of the soul. It would seem to be true that although we can disguise our body language in many ways, it is less easy to disguise the feelings our eyes express. We all know of people who 'smile with their mouths' – usually people in the public eye such as politicians, whose broad grins are given the lie by the lack of warmth in the eyes. It is said that there are over 50 different types of human smile. It is possible or scientists to tell if a smile is sincere or not by analysing the movements involved in a smile, which is the work of over 80 muscles in the face. In a real smile, the eyes tend to smile with the mouth. This is indicated by a small amount of wrinkling around the eyes. If this is missing then the smile is probably false.

Dogs are pack animals, and in the canine world eye contact between dogs is a sign of aggression. Try staring a dog out. If the dog recognises your 'superiority' he will avoid your direct gaze and drop his eyes; a dog who stares you out may well be hostile.

In the more complex human world, we tend – at least in Western cultures – to equate eye contact with honesty and confidence, particularly if the eye contact is accompanied by a smile, or at least a relaxed facial expression. In other cultures, for instance in Japan, direct eye contact may be regarded as rude, and is totally unacceptable in women (that is, direct eye contact between men and women).

The eyes are tremendously important for communicating with other people. For example,

Eye contact

when we disagree with someone we say that we cannot see "eye-to-eye" with them to convey the lack of empathy we feel that we have with them. When we first meet some people we feel instantly at ease and comfortable with them. However, other people can make us feel completely uncomfortable. This tendency to get on with some people better than others can usually be explained by the length of time that they look at us or they way that they hold our gaze as they speak. When someone that we are talking to is being less than honest is concealing something from us, his eyes maintain our gaze for less than one-third of the time.

It is thought that when we drop our gaze below the eye-level of the person that we are speaking to, it tends to create a social atmosphere. Below the eye-level is somewhere between the mouth. It is a common trick of police interrogators to go below the eye-level of the suspect they are questioning. This helps create a more relaxed and friendly atmosphere and means that the person who is being questioned is more likely to confide in them. When you are a conference, you can maintain a formal atmosphere by making sure that you keep your gaze above the other people's eye-levels.

Eye contact can be a difficult form of body language to modify because it is hard to get the balance right and to tell when you are giving someone too much eye contact or too little when they are talking to you. It is imperative to achieve the correct balance between looking at someone enough and looking too much. It has been shown that if we stare too long at someone this is interpreted negatively and makes that person feel uncomfortable. Therefore, while we enjoy a certain level of eye-contact, too much can be worse than too little and when people stare at us it makes us uncomfortable.

If a person is not speaking to you or you them, it is better not to look at them. Making eye contact with someone when you are not actually speaking to them can make the person feel very uncomfortable and you may give them a bad impression. It is difficult to control your gaze, but with a little practise and monitoring, it can be kept under control.

We have a tendency to judge other people by the amount of and the type of eye contact we have with them. Research has shown that we are more likely both to look at and to maintain eye-contact with people that we like. It follows then that if someone makes quite a bit of eye-contact with us the we feel that they are showing that they like us and we are more likely to respond positively to them. It is also said that a low-level of eye-contact is interpreted as someone not paying attention whilst a high level of eye-contact is often taken to mean that the person is being sincere. Studies have also shown that men are

Eye contact

less likely to find women attractive if they do not make eye-contact with them. Women, however, are said to be more interested in a man who does not make eye-contact with them. This could explain the theory behind "playing hard to get".

Pointing at someone whilst making eye contact with someone else may appear to the person you are pointing at that you are talking about them so it is best not to do it. Even if you are pointing at the person that you are talking to and making eye contact with, this can be interpreted as aggressive as having someone's eyes and finger singling you out is overbearing.

Whilst overdoing eye contact can give offence or can make other people uncomfortable, it is necessary to make come eye contact when we are talking to someone else. When we are doing so, it is worth bearing in mind the following guidelines. If you look at someone for less than one third of the time may be communicating that you are shy, particularly if you keep looking at the ground. If the person doesn't know you that well, they may attribute this inability to make eye contact as a sign that you are lying to them, especially if you keep looking from side-to side. However, if you look at someone's eyes for more that two thirds of the time, it may communicate to them that you have a soft spot for them or that you are being rather aggressive. If you give constant eye contact and do not look away at all then this can be interpreted as you are being aggressive – i.e., you are trying to stare them out. It can also mean that you are attracted to them. The degree to which we make eye contact is a factor that varies from culture to culture. In Mediterranean countries people tend to make more eye contact than they do in Britain where people are much less open about their feelings.

The cliché of the shifty-eyed car salesman has its core of truth: when someone is trying to sell us something, we need to see their eyes. This is obviously affected by the context that we are in. In a business situation or when something is being sold to us,, we are more likely to suspect that someone who cannot meet your gaze – who shifts his eyes sideways or downwards, or fixes on a point directly behind your ear – is not telling the truth.

There is, however, a limit to the time we can make direct eye contact with other people. If you and a friend are sitting opposite each other chatting over a coffee, it is normal that periods of direct eye contact will be followed by 'rest' periods when the gaze moves away, looking across the room or at the table. Other aspects of body language (for example, bending towards the other person) indicate that you are still interested in them, and vice versa. If, after a reasonable length of time, your friend's eyes do not come back to you, you may assume the conversation

Eye contact

is over and they are thinking that it's time to go.

It is also worth remembering that there are reasons other than lying why people may not meet your direct gaze. One is intense emotion. If someone is describing to you a very painful event, such as the death of a loved one, they will be unable to look you in the eye while doing so. Another is if somebody is remembering something it is literally hard for them to remember, that is, difficult to recollect. The reason for this is that intense emotion and the act of memory both drive us inward; it's as if we're searching our inner selves, trying to connect with memories and feelings deep within our private inner core. The intensity of this communication with the inner self means that it is not possible to look at (i.e., focus on) another, outside being. This is why in most religions the act of prayer is done with eyes closed, so that the individual can more easily retreat within himself, without being distracted by the external world.

Eye contact indicates warmth and interest. If we meet someone at a party who engages our eyes and appears to look deep inside them for more than the requisite period of time, we think they're interested in us and tend to find them attractive. Men and women, when asked why they found X so attractive, often reply along the lines of: 'He/she treated me as if I was the only person in the room. He/she just gazed into my eyes the whole time'. This interest may well be genuine; it may also be a practised seduction technique. (The same is true of sales people too of course: if you're selling shoddy or poor merchandise, make sure you practice holding eye contact beforehand!) Rudolf Valentino became a sex symbol of the silent screen because of his dark, brooding, penetrating gaze – women must have yearned for the penetration to be by other parts of his anatomy as well. While that may be irresistible on the big screen for a few minutes, in real life it can be unsettling if not downright threatening.

The worst thing you can do at a party, when introduced to someone, is never to make eye contact, or make only brief eye contact when introduced, and thereafter talk at the other person while letting your eyes wander around the room at all the other guests. This is so rude that you might as well make the V-sign at the other person and have done with it: you are in effect dominating them (by continuing to talk, so they can't make away) while invalidating their existence by refusing them eye contact.

Eye contact is affirmation: it means, 'I recognise you, I see you exist, I acknowledge your reality.' Refusing eye contact says: 'You are invisible, you might just as well not be there.' If we are seen to shut our eyes for a few seconds or begin to avoid eye-contact with someone it generally means that we are bored or annoyed and that we do not want to have to

Eye contact

listen to that person speak any longer.

In business or interview situations, we tend to like the person who strides into the room with a confident smile, makes pleasant but not penetrating eye contact, and who, during the interview, regularly makes eye contact with the other people in the room but does allow the eyes to dart from person to person in a light, interested fashion.

The role of eye contact in aggression is well known. When children play 'staring out' games – staring at each other to see who 'breaks' first and looks away – they are unconsciously acknowledging this. If you are male and you walk into a pub and deliberately stare at another man (assuming it's a heterosexual situation) and the other man may well soon come over and demand 'What's up with you, pal?' In a male-oriented world, dominated by notions of power and status, a fixed stare from male to male can often be the prelude to a punch-up.

Deference to a monarch has taken many traditional forms: bowing and curtseying are obvious forms (thereby lowering or making oneself physically inferior to the monarch), but it is only in modern times that it has been 'OK' to look straight at a king or queen, or some other senior royal. In the past, etiquette demanded that, in the presence of the sovereign, subjects should look down slightly, or to the side, thus emphasising their inferiority and subject status.

In many religions, and in the autocratic monarchies of myth and legend, looking upon the face of God or the face of the monarch was punishable by death. Ordinary mortals simply could not fix their eyes directly on something sacred or all-powerful without being punished.

The role of eye contact in seduction has been mentioned above. Making eye contact with someone in whom you are sexually interested is one of the first and most common ways of attracting their attention; the eyes can give the other person signals to which they can respond. How often have you heard an exchange similar to this one?

A: Do you think there's anything going on between Jack and Lucy?
B: What makes you say that?
A: Well, he keeps looking at her when she's not looking at him....

When we first experience attraction to another person, it's as if we cannot get enough of their physical appearance: we want to drink them in with the eyes, looking at them constantly, whether or not that gaze is returned. Traditionally, lovers are two people who can sit or lie for hours on end, just looking at each other, as if we could enter inside

Eye contact

another person simply by searching their eyes for clues to their heart.

We can interpret the health or not of a relationship by the number of times a couple look at each other in public. Couples who, in social situations, avoid the gaze of the other or simply ignore it, may have lost the spark they once had.

Winking is an eye gesture that is now often derided as the mark of a phoney (and it often is). A wink indicates a secret shared, or a private joke. If one person winks at another behind the back of a third, it is because those two people share a secret or have hatched a plot concerning the third. During a business meeting, if colleagues attract each other's eyes, one of them may wink at the other to indicate something only the two of them know or feel: 'Oh God, he's off again on his favourite soapbox', 'I see he's wearing that egg-stained tie again' or 'Never mind, soon be 5 o'clock'.

In terms of a sexual come-on, it is usually men who wink at women: the man is indicating that he feels that he and the woman share a personal secret, which is their connection with each other – or what he would like to be their connection. When screen stars like Marlene Dietrich or Lauren Bacall winked in movies, it was a sign of their rakish, tough, femme fatale qualities, but in practice winking by women was seen as 'unwomanly'.

The man who winks too much is as much an object of scorn as the wolf-whistler; typically, the serial winker is the slob in the corner at parties, hopelessly unattractive, winking at any female unfortunate enough to catch his eye and whom he thinks will fall under his spell. They are almost always disappointed, and quite right too.

CHAPTER 9
Standing or sitting: the top dog

We use words like 'the head' or the 'the top job' when we are talking about people or positions of authority, as in 'the head teacher', 'the head of his department', the 'top consultant'. Height and physical supremacy imply power.

If you are sitting down, someone who is standing close to you is 'superior' or a threat: you are in the submissive role. There can be few body positions more threatening that the boss or teacher who leans with his/her arms on the desk of a seated person, particularly if they are putting their face too close to that of the other person. Leaning over someone is a direct threat: unless, that is, they have invited you to do so: even then, there is the implication that you (the inferior) has invited the standing person (the superior) to check or validate what you are doing.

If you need to lean over the desk of another person, pull up a chair to make sure that you are literally on their level. If the desk or table is a large one, it helps if two people sit together at one end or corner of that table: such a position indicates that they are 'on the same side'. Neither is in a superior position, and so any sense of threat may be removed. Be aware that once you quite literally 'tower over' another person you are intimidating them. If this is your intention, then perhaps you should question why it is that why you need to do this: all it serves to do is to put people on the defensive, and is rarely seen to be productive.

The situations can be reversed, however, and the unequal power structure maintained. Think of a schoolboy being called to the head teacher's office, or an employee being 'carpeted' (literally, standing on the carpet) by the boss. The schoolboy or the employee is standing, but the authority figure is seated. The seated figure maintains control in two ways: first, they are almost always seated behind a desk (protection, a symbol of power) while the other is not (they have no physical defences); second, the standing figure is required to remain still. The schoolboy may not wander around the room or change his position while being told off: he must stay in one place, at the whim of the seated figure who in contrast is in a relaxed and comfortable position. Standing upright for any length of time is tiring and unnatural, and when you force people to do this you

Standing or sitting: the top dog

are both inflicting discomfort on them and placing them at a disadvantage.

It has also been observed that the greater status or power a person has, the less body language they need. A man seated behind a desk need only say, "no" quietly, confident in the knowledge that his words will be obeyed; it is only the less powerful that feel the need to use body language ("I really need this chance", perhaps while wringing the hands to show frustration or desperation). The more acute our situation, the more visual the body language – taken to extremes, we can perhaps think of the person being physically attacked, and warding off blows with his arms.

The seated figure can alter his or her position in a number of ways: push his chair back on two legs, put his hands in his pockets, put his hands behind his head, lean back – all these indicate relaxed confidence and power.

Modern management studies place great importance on the arrangement of furniture in rooms to avoid unequal body positions. For example, a manager may have a desk in his office to work at, but he or she will have another area with more comfortable chairs and no table (or a low coffee table) at which he or she can sit to chat with employees in a more informal manner. They are both thus at the same level, with no authority symbols or barriers such as a desk between them. It is very difficult to be aggressive and seek to dominate people in such circumstances: when we want to dominate it is instinctive that we seek to be 'higher' than the other person.

Most companies have a rectangular boardroom table, with those in highest authority seated in the 'top' position at the 'head' of the table; your status is reflected in high how up the table you are seated. More modern management strategies, which seek equality rather than a hierarchical culture, prefer round tables (as did King Arthur, who sought to pacify his squabbling knights by using a round table) with no seating order, or a loosely circular configuration of low comfy chairs on which to hold meetings.

The medical profession is also beginning to understand the importance of body language. Traditionally, the doctor (the Wise Man, powerful and

Standing or sitting: the top dog

the possessor of knowledge) sits behind his desk with the patient's notes in front of him – the notes (the patient's secrets) are hidden from the patient himself, who sits in the submissive position in front of the desk. Today, with notions of accountability becoming more widely accepted – not to mention fear of litigation – doctors seek to develop a better 'working partnership' with their patients.

In the situation described above – an employee standing in front of a seated authority figure – the balance of power would shift dramatically if the standing person leaned against something.

Sitting side-by-side is a sign of equality and companionship.

Because, as I said, standing upright is tiring, we almost always look for something – a door, a table, a wall – to lean against. The leaning person will then adopt a position with their arms which further relaxes the situation and reasserts their authority. The two most common positions are to fold the arms (a defensive or aggressive posture, see the section on arm positions) or (for men) to put their hands in their pockets, which may be either a gesture of complete relaxation or a way of establishing either equality or superiority to the other person. (Depending on context, it could also even be vaguely threatening: we've already seen how open hands away from the body suggest the honesty of not being armed; hands in pockets by contrast can imply secrecy, leading us to wonder if that person has a 'weapon' they're waiting to use on us.)

We also lean against things to assert ownership – for example, leaning against your car or garden wall is a way of drawing attention to your personal property (and thus your level of prestige) and saying 'This is mine, I own it'. Society being what it is, while you might often see men leaning against the bonnet of a Porsche or a Lexus, they are less likely to claim identification with a small (= less sexual charisma) or less upmarket car. When a man and a woman who are involved with each other are sitting on a sofa, the man will often place his arm along the back of the sofa, behind the women. This is significant of 'ownership', a way of saying 'Mine'. When this is done by men as part of a sexual advance, women quite rightly find it offensive: the woman may lean forward or move away from the arm altogether. as if to say 'You've no right to claim ownership until I say so.'

The subtext of such body language is, of course, insecurity. We are all familiar with the cliché of the unattractive, perhaps physically small man (in a world where height = power) with little social charm who buys the biggest, fastest, flashiest car around: men who secretly or subconsciously perceive themselves as inadequate often compensate in this way. The man who doesn't feel the need to lean against his less flashy car, or demonstrate ownership of his wife or girlfriend by the arm against the back of the sofa, may not be unaware of social status or body language – it is just that he is sufficiently self-confident not to need to advertise himself in this way.

The female equivalent of such crossed messages would be the woman who provocatively draws attention to her physical attractiveness in public: crossing and uncrossing her legs, for example, or patting her hair, or wearing overtly sexy clothes. There may be an underlying insecurity that is compensated for by an overt appearance of sexuality that is designed to appeal to men.

In the days before self-service, when petrol stations employed staff to fill cars up with fuel, it was widely observed and accepted that whereas women would remain in their cars, roll down the window and ask for the amount of petrol they wanted, men would get out of the car and oversee the pump attendant's work, typically standing by with hands in pockets (suggest relaxation and/or 'secret power') or wandering around the car while it was being filled. It is generally accepted that men identify with their cars far more than women do, in many cases regarding their car as an extension of their personalities and a badge of their status in society. It's understandable, therefore, that men could not remain seated (that is, in an inferior or vulnerable position) 'trapped' inside their cars, while a third party who was standing (and therefore dominant) performed some 'aggressive' (some would say positively sexual) act upon the car!

Chapter 10
Arms and the man (and woman)

In the next two sections, we look at how our arms and our legs, the limbs of the body, express our inner feelings. As they are extensions of the main limb, hands and feet are also included.

Crudely put, our body language can be either open or closed. 'Open' indicates that the person is relaxed, confident, interested, calm. 'Closed' body language involves all those gestures that can indicate aggression, nervousness, anxiety or antipathy.

The terms are self-explanatory: a person whose body language is closed will often have their legs and arms crossed, and seem to be hugging themselves, or hunched in an attempt to close themselves down and in. It's the physical equivalent of battening down the hatches: prepared for fight or flight, they are tense and on edge.

Open body language is literally that – arms often away from the body, palms open, legs comfortable.

Folded arms across the chest. We all do this, and in almost every situation every day you can see other people doing this. What does it mean?

By folding your arms across your chest, you are creating a barrier between yourself and other people. Barriers are, of course, both defensive and offensive: they are for protection, but also evidence of a hostile environment.

The firmer the grip, the greater the degree of tension or aggression.

We fold our arms as a protection so that the outside world won't see what we're really like inside, a mass of insecurities and doubts. But a barrier also hides, obscures and prevents things getting through: an interesting piece of research compared two groups of students who were given the same tutorial with the same information. One group were instructed to listen to the lecture with arms folded and legs crossed; the other group were instructed to sit in an 'open' position. The results revealed that the students who had adopted the open sitting position retained 38 per cent more of the information given to them that the group who sat tightly hunched and 'closed'.

This suggests therefore that if we wish to alter our personalities or capabilities, we might start with consciously adapting our body language. People who habitually fold their arms would say 'It's more comfortable that way'. Psychological research has

Arms and the man (and woman)

shown that people can be 'comfortable' even with negative or damaging circumstances, since 'comfortable' only means that which we're used to. (Taken to an extreme, it explains why abused children show such loyalty to their abusers: it is all they know, and are 'comfortable' with). In other words, folding our arms to form a barrier is comfortable for us because we are used to the habitual negative, defensive feelings of which they are evidence. If we sought to develop positive aspects of our lives and character, we'd feel less and less the need to barrier ourselves.

None of which is to say that there won't always be moments in our lives when arm-folding is comfortable – waiting for a job interview, for instance, or for an appointment with the dentist or doctor. Arm-folding reflects our inner tension and anxiety at such moments.

Typically, we fold our arms when listening to someone with whom we disagree or to whom we feel hostile. Just as soldiers faced with an enemy erect a defensive-offensive barricade, so we fold our arms to place distance between ourselves and 'the enemy'.

Women have alternative

forms of arm-folding, using their handbags to create a barrier between themselves and others. Usually, men carry little if anything about with them, tradition dictating that their immediate necessities such as cash can be carried in their pockets. If they do carry something such as a briefcase this can be carried at the side, almost like a weapon. By contrast, women carry their essential items in a separate container which is either draped over them or carried in the hand, thus limiting their freedom of movement and creating a barrier against the world. An extraordinary example of this is Her Majesty the Queen and her famous handbags: stiff, unyielding accessories draped over one arm. She has no need to carry keys or money or shopping lists or mobile phones about with her – what is the handbag for?

Partial arm-cross. This is typically a female gesture, and involves crossing one arm across the body (usually across the vulnerable stomach/womb area) and holding on to the other arm which lies straight at their side. This has been interpreted as a gesture of self-giving comfort, a gesture of reassuring oneself. The human and animal behaviourist

Arms and the man (and woman)

Desmond Morris has written that when adults do this they are recreating the feeling of security experienced as children when a parent held their hand.

Hands behind the back. Walking with the hands clasped behind the back is usually associated with male members of the British Royal Family. In fact, it is often seen in men in positions of power or authority, such as senior army officers or policemen on the beat who are not carrying weapons (see below). Unsurprisingly, this denotes confidence and power: the man is saying 'I am invulnerable'.

Armed soldiers or policemen (who are not actually carrying their weapons) will tend to stand and walk with their arms by their sides, ready for action. Carrying the arms loosely by the side is also a sign of confidence: and, indeed, an armed person will usually feel confident. Those who carry weapons (or senior army officers and policemen who carry batons) do so in the classic way with the weapon projecting from the body like a substitute erect penis. It's the most sensible way of carrying weapons, of course, which is why they do it, but we should not escape the analogy with male power and force.

Hand on heart. This body language can have a variety of meanings. At its apparent level, it means 'I am telling the truth' just as with 'Cross my heart and hope to die'. When we use the phrase 'to speak from

GUIDE TO BODY LANGUAGE

the heart', we imply truth-telling and sincerity: we are speaking from the core of our being. It is, however, a complex gesture, and the cluster of behaviours around it need to be studied.

For instance, in someone seeking to divert blame from themselves, the gesture also means 'It wasn't me'. When a teacher says 'It was you, wasn't it?' the guilty pupil may open their eyes wide to indicate surprise and place a hand on their heart: 'It wasn't me'. The gesture is protective of the self, but is also draws attention to the 'innocent party'.

As with other body language, all the signals have to checked. A salesperson who says 'Trust me on this one', with hand on heart but eyes looking elsewhere, needs to be treated with caution. (See Conscious and unconscious body language, the section on Verbal highlighting.)

Hands on hips. A person who stands with their hands on their hips, elbows almost level with shoulders, is literally making themselves bigger: they are occupying more space than other people. It is thus a gesture signifying power, confidence, authority and readiness – it's the way a gunfighter might stand,

Arms and the man (and woman)

showing he's ready to reach for his gun, ready for action. It's a position often adopted by athletes waiting for the race to start, or footballers waiting for the whistle to blow; people of strength and physical prowess who are happy to have their bodies looked at.

In the sport of rugby, the New Zealand All-Blacks team start each international match with a haka – a Maori ritual in which they face their opponents, make eye contact, and perform a traditional dance full of intimidating body language: stamping of feet, waving of arms, lunging and diving and standing with the legs splayed (thus emphasising their dominant sexuality): all gestures suggesting fearlessness, courage and absolute dominance over their opponents.

There's only one way for an opposing team to take the haka, and it's interesting to watch how many teams do so: face the All-Blacks, return that steady and firm eye contact – and stand with hands on hips, in a gesture of defiance and come-and-get-me-if-you-think-you're-so-hard.

In interactions between men and women who are sexually attracted to one another, it is also a come-on (as is standing with one hand only on the hip). The person standing with hands on hips is basically saying to the other 'Come and get me. I'm available', while drawing attention to their body (and specifically, because the hands are placed near them) the sexual organs. This is why it is one of the classic poses adopted by nude models or the models in pornographic magazines: the arms will typically either be held away from the body or placed near erogenous zones.

Arms around other people. This is generally interpreted as a display of affection. In its gentlest form, it displays a desire to protect and care for – as when we seek to comfort a grieving person or a hurt child. We place one or both arms round the other person to offer them shelter and also to create a barrier between them and their hurt.

It is also a symbol of ownership. Lovers, typically, walk or stand with their arms round one another. This says: 'This is mine. Don't touch'. Between lovers, touching through clothes in this manner is also one of the only socially acceptable forms of contact they can have in public.

We have all had experiences of recoiling when people whom we don't want to put their arms round us. Think of the office party, when drunken bozos chance their arm (quite literally) by throwing their limbs around the women they work with. This is

Arms and the man (and woman)

offensive, but not necessarily because it's a sexual come-on (which it may not be). It's offensive because this person is claiming possession of us, saying in body language 'This is mine' when that's the last thing we want.

As has been stated earlier on several occasions, we need to be aware of cultural differences where body language is concerned. In some cultures, any form of physical contact between members of the opposite sex who are not related is absolutely taboo. British people have traditionally been less inclined to touch each other while speaking. We have also historically been inclined to believe that any men or women who touch each other must be sexually involved, as physical contact between those not sexually involved was taboo. In France, for instance, it's quite common for girls or women who are platonic friends to link arms or have their arms round each other's shoulders when walking down the street. It does not mean that they are lesbians; it is simply a sign of friendship. Many British women may think a woman friend was making a sexual advance if she attempted similar behaviour, but that is simply the British attitude towards touching.

Touching people while speaking (usually by placing the hand on the arm of the other person) is something seen widely in Mediterranean countries. It can be a means of emphasising your words, or underlining them; it can be a way of ensuring that you have the listener's full attention. Many people think that a person who touches others easily is warm and sincere: after all, we usually avoid touching people whom we do not like. Others find it totally unacceptable and recoil from it. I remember a colleague years ago complaining that an American friend of ours 'always has to touch everyone all the time – I hate it'. The touches in question were light gestures on the arm or the shoulder; I suspect the real reason for my colleague's dislike of this was that he felt, subconsciously or consciously, that the woman was making a dominant sexual play for him (she wasn't) and he was rejecting this.

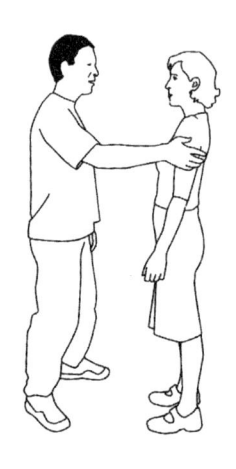

Touching the back or the stomach. This behaviour is often (though not by any means always) seen in men towards the women for whom they care. The two most vulnerable parts of the human body are the back (because we can't reach it) and the stomach, the solar plexus: in Eastern philosophy, the core of our

Arms and the man (and woman)

being. In language, we talk about a 'stab in the back' or a 'kick in the stomach' as being two of the most wounding things that could happen to us, things that really hurt us in our most vulnerable places.

A finger or a hand poked at the back in a pushing gesture is aggressive and hostile; the same with a finger or a hand poked at the stomach. In society, such hostility would often be the prelude to a fight.

The palm of the hand placed gently against the back of another is an encouraging, gentle, caring gesture; we often do this to comfort the grief-stricken. Placing the flat of the palm against the stomach of another is usually reserved for those in a close relationship – it is an extremely intimate gesture, most often seen in men who touch the stomachs of their partners as a gesture of protection or love for the unborn child who may be there.

CHAPTER 11
The language of legs

Almost all the comments made above about arms (crossing or folding, creating barriers, indicating anxiety or defensiveness) apply to the legs as well. Legs and arms usually mirror each other: a person sitting with their arms tightly folded is likely to have their legs crossed too, and unlikely to have their legs slightly apart in a relaxed, open position.

Crossed legs are not just a barrier against the world; importantly, they defend the sexual areas in both men and women, and so are a protective gesture.

It should also be stated that crossing the legs is actually part of a comfortable repertoire of ways in which to sit (although see comments made above about arms). Most people, while sitting for a long period of time, will at some stage cross and re-cross their legs, although they will also stretch them out, or cross them at the ankles.

Repeated crossing and uncrossing of legs is interpreted as a sign of boredom, typically seen during speeches or over-long public ceremonies. The sitter is saying they want to get up and go.

Crossing the legs – often in conjunction with folded arms – is a sign of withdrawal or displeasure. The person is disassociating themselves from something or showing their displeasure at the proceedings. Check the platform at the next round of party political conferences. Those with arms and legs tightly crossed are in effect saying: 'This is nothing to do with me and I wish I wasn't here'.

The language of legs

What women do with their legs is to some extent dictated by fashion and skirt-length, although to that must be added the observation that women have choice over how they dress, and are thus making a statement about their personality in that way. Short skirts mean that for 'modesty's' sake women wearing them often tend not to cross their legs but instead sit with their knees together or their legs crossed at the ankles; a woman wearing a short skirt who nevertheless crosses her legs may well be adopting that pose for negative, defensive reasons – she could also be sending out sexual signals.

The legs, after all, are part of a woman's sexual 'armoury'. Men are described as being 'leg men' or 'breast men', referring to the part of the female anatomy by which they judge the rest, and on which depends their sexual judgement of the female as attractive or not. In the body language of sexual attraction, people try to draw attention to the part of the body they want the other to notice, and crossing legs in a short skirt is an obvious way of getting them noticed.

An interesting fashion trend from the 1990s onwards was the popularity of opaque black tights. These meant that women could have their cake and eat it too: wearing very short skirts with opaque tights means that the shape and length of the legs is visible, but the 'flesh' (that is, the sexual part) is invisible.

This reflects an unconscious desire on the part of women to be liberated in their choice of dress but also to retain their own mystique and privacy.

Sitting with knees together. Since the advent of shorter skirts in the twentieth century, sitting with the knees pressed together and feet neatly together has been the 'ladylike' position for women to adopt. It is not particularly comfortable and cannot be maintained for long, but that in itself should say something about the place of women in society and the behaviour expected of them. 'Nice' women should not sit in a way that exposes too much flesh or draws attention to themselves. Nowadays, it is unusual to see women under the age of 45 or so sitting like this, and certainly no woman who has been influenced by the feminist revolution.

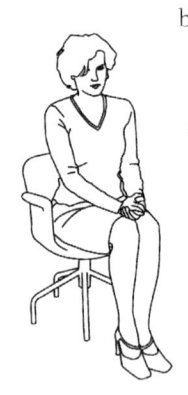

During the later part of the twentieth century it became socially acceptable for women to wear trousers in all walks of life: emulating the male business suit (the unremarkable, unimaginative uniform of the working man), the trouser suit became a normal part of most women's wardrobes. By wearing

The language of legs

it women were not only saying they were the equals of men and wanting to take their place in a man's world (perhaps at the loss of some of their individuality?) but also that in wearing trousers they could sit and walk and move in a freer, less constricted way. A whole repertoire of movement (and body language) is available to a woman in trousers that is denied to a woman wearing, for example, a short or tight skirt.

The American leg-cross. Most often seen in the US and familiar from films and TV, this involves resting the ankle or lower calf of one leg across the other knee. It is very much associated with the relaxed, easy style associated with American culture – and with the competitiveness and pace of American life. It may look relaxed but that, in a sense, puts the other person off their guard. In terms of body language, the body is held back while the feet (for kicking and walking) are thrust forward and the body is 'closed' by the position of the supported leg. It's the attitude of someone ready to argue their corner to the very end.

When a man is sitting in this position and additionally holding the supported leg in a clamp, you may be sure that you are dealing with a very stubborn and determined customer indeed.

The ankle-lock. As may be guessed, this is a defensive position. Women tend to lock ankles with knees pressed together by crossing their ankles over each other; men will often sit with knees apart but ankles crossed. This is a negative and defensive posture. If you could look under the table at a board meeting, or a Cabinet meeting even, you would see many feet in this position – prepared for attack and ready to defend themselves.

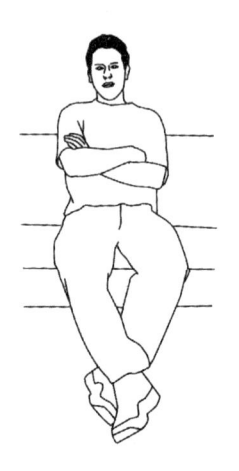

Sitting with legs wide apart. This has been discussed in the section on personal space. This position is adopted mostly by men, although of course it is perfectly possible for women wearing trousers who want to make a point. Because it makes the body wider than it is, it is an arrogant, aggressive gesture, typical of the macho, dominant male. There

The language of legs

is also of course a sexual overtone to the pose: a man trying to attract a woman might sit like this as a come-on – effectively showing what he's got and suggesting its availability. A woman wearing jeans or trousers would do so for the same reason, revealing her (covered) vaginal area but by adopting a usually masculine pose also suggesting combativeness and an aggressive sexuality that men would find attractive. A woman using this method of attracting sexual notice would tend not to sit still, though, and will often have one leg raised with the heel tucked in near her bottom so that she can hold her arms around it – another piece of body language suggesting desire and availability.

Sitting on the edge of your seat. Almost universally accepted as a sign of being ill-at-ease. Relaxed people in their own environments tend to sit back on a chair; in fact few people in their own homes actually sit on chairs, they tend to lie or sprawl or drape themselves across the chairs, perhaps with legs tucked under them or hanging over the side of a chair or sofa. Tense people, uncertain of their own situation, sit on the edge of the

145

chair: it also suggests the person may not really want to be there, and is ready to leave. At job interviews, candidates seldom sit right back in the chair: it's as if they're poised for flight, but also that they're taking nothing for granted. We use the phrase 'He's got his feet under the table' to suggest that a person is making themselves at home and, by extension, taking advantage of a situation. Candidates wanting to impress prospective employers will not want to give the impression that they are taking anything for granted.

Leg and foot direction. It's often said that when people are sitting or standing, their feet usually point in the direction they want to go. In reading body language, this is useful in social situations. For instance, if a person is standing and talking to you, but angling one or both feet away from you, it's reasonable to infer that they are looking for an excuse to go. This is particularly noticeable if two acquaintances meet by accident in the street and one of them is anxious to make a getaway: his or her face and upper body may be facing the person who is detaining them, but legs and/or feet will be pointing away, ready to make an escape.

When two people are sitting chatting on a sofa, or on two chairs close to each other, their faces and upper bodies may suggest closeness, as they bend

The language of legs

forward to listen to each other, but the angle of the legs and feet may tell another story. If the legs and feet of one or both persons are pointing away from the person they are talking to, they are in effect saying they want to get away.

Foot-tapping and stamping. Foot-tapping is a standard way of expressing irritability and impatience; the foot taps to suggest that the pace should speed up a bit, and things should happen. Stamping, thankfully, is seldom seen beyond toddlerhood, being the typical behaviour of a toddler who, goaded to tears of rage and frustration, cannot have exactly what he or she wants. The movement suggests that the person would like to stamp on your head if you don't do exactly what they want! It attracts attention and suggests violence, and that's what it's for.

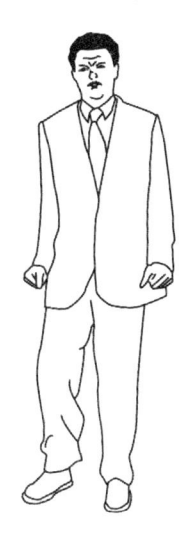

Standing cross-legged. Particularly if the arms are crossed too, this is a very defensive posture, and is often seen at parties or in social situations where people feel insecure. If you held a party and invited a dozen people who were complete strangers to one another, you would find at the beginning of the party that a high proportion were standing with legs and arms crossed, protecting themselves. As they gradually got to know one another and the drink flowed, you would see the legs and arms uncrossing and the body language suggesting an opening up, an expansion.

At an office party where everybody knows everyone else, only the very shy or insecure members of staff would cross arms and legs (perhaps particularly if talking to the boss). They would also stand in the corner or on the periphery of the group, seeking not to be noticed. By contrast, you will hardly ever see a senior manager cross arms or legs in such a situation and almost certainly he or she will not stand anywhere but in the centre of the room. He may, however, cross his arms to show his disapproval of the goings on, or his dislike of what is being said to him!

CHAPTER 12
Head, face and neck language

As with all comments on body language, it's worth stating yet again that so much depends on individual context, and that rather than looking at one gesture alone, the language of the whole body should be studied. To give an example: it is widely accepted that covering the mouth while speaking indicates deceit or obfuscation, if not downright lying. Other factors may be involved. It is particularly true of women, for instance, that if they feel insecure about a bodily or facial part (and women are more often insecure about themselves than men) they will try to hide it, sometimes unconsciously. A woman who, while talking to you, repeatedly brings her hand near her mouth, or seems to want to cover her mouth, may be absolutely truthful: she may also think that she has a protruding or unsightly set of teeth, and be trying to hide these from you because she wants you to find her attractive.

The hair

People who touch, pat or stroke their hair are often seeking reassurance. It may be an unconscious reminder of the way in which a consoling parent smooths a child's head to comfort them.

Variations on this – often intensely irritating to those who have to watch it – are hair twisting or hair chewing. As they usually have much longer hair and can actually get at it, girls and women are more prone to this. As with any repetitious movement such as chewing or sucking (of which it may be an unconscious reminder) twisting hair brings temporary release to the highly anxious person; however, as with nail biting, it is addictive behaviour and a habit hard to break. Nail biters will often chew their nails until they bleed or are extremely sore in an attempt to soothe themselves, hair twisters can end up pulling out whole clumps of hair. They won't be able to stop until they realise that they are exhibiting nervous behaviour, and find a resolution of that anxiety or channel it into different directions. It has even been suggested that

Head, face and neck language

people who chew nails or twist hair as children are much more likely, as adults, to become dependent on cigarettes, alcohol or drugs.

Running your fingers through the hair of someone else is an intimate sexual gesture, as is any gesture involving one person touching the face of another. There seem to be three zones of touching: touching the back, arm, head or shoulder of another person can be simply a gesture of platonic friendship or liking; touching the breasts or genital area is, obviously, a frankly sexual gesture. In between these extremes comes the face, an ambiguous territory bordering on the intimate. We seldom want to touch the face of someone we don't feel great affection for (except perhaps to slap it!) but people who feel strong physical attraction for each other will usually find any excuse to touch the object of their desire somewhere on the face. If people are fully clothed, it is the most naked part of the body; touching the face is therefore a substitute for touching the other person's naked body.

Running your fingers through your own hair (particularly if a tugging or violent movement is involved) generally indicates intolerable frustration or exasperation. It's the action of an overworked, harassed executive just told to go back and do the sales forecast yet again.

In the context of sexual attraction, a woman may run her fingers through her own hair to emphasise its length and beauty for the benefit of a man whom she finds appealing. This behaviour may be conscious or unconscious. It is typically a female behaviour, as male hair is nowadays not typically regarded as an important part of their sexual allure!

Head, face and neck language

The head

In most Western countries (though not in all) nodding the head up and down signifies agreement and shaking the head from side to side signifies disagreement. As described earlier, in Greece a slight upward tilt of the head and eyebrows is 'no'.

When two people are having a conversation, or a group of people are talking, head movements help to keep the meeting lively and two-way, or to keep all the participants involved. For instance, someone listening to a friend recounting a story will frequently nod or shake their head (often accompanied by verbal sounds such as 'mmm') to give encouragement to continue and to reassure the speaker that they are still listening and still engaged with the narrative. At a business meeting round a table, the person speaking will hope to see his or her colleagues occasionally nod or shake their heads – again, to indicate interest and encouragement, or at least prove they have not fallen asleep.

Tossing the head backwards, rather like a restive horse, can indicate boredom or restlessness or frank disagreement. If you were trying to sell a product or an idea to someone who kept tossing their head, especially if they avoided eye contact with you, you would do well to change tactics or beat a hasty retreat. In a sexual context, a woman tossing her head in the presence of a man she finds attractive will be sending out unconscious signals about the beauty of her head and/or hair for the man to notice.

When someone puts the palm of their hand up to support the side of their face (often round a table, with the elbow on the table) beware – the sign says 'Extreme Boredom'. It's as if the hand is keeping the face upright, and without this support it would fall forward, sound asleep. If you are trying to persuade a colleague of something or gain someone's agreement and you see them do this, then you know for sure you are not succeeding.

If, however, the head is 'supported' by an index finger against the side of the head, then evaluation is taking place. It's as if the index (the most important finger) is making direct contact with the brain, seeking an answer.

Chin-stroking, or chin-holding, is usually associated with the process of making a decision. A salesperson who observes this in a potential client knows, therefore, that they are taking the pitch seriously, even if the answer will then be 'no' (which they can gauge by whether or not the person then seems anxious to move away or not).

Head, face and neck language

The mouth

If someone is talking to you and they place their hand, or fingers, or even a clenched fist over their mouth, pay attention. They may be telling you a downright lie. They may not be telling you the exact truth. For instance, if you ask a friend 'Are you feeling OK?' and they untruthfully say 'Yes, fine' this is a lie in the starkest meaning of the word, but the kind of lie we regard as socially acceptable, often told out of a desire to spare others or save a situation. Teachers should be concerned if, when they ask their pupils 'Did you understand that?', some pupils have their hands covering their mouths when they nod 'yes'. That is the moment to respond with: 'Does anyone have any questions?' to allow those who did not understand to air their misgivings.

A person may place their hand over their mouth when they are speaking of something painful or distasteful. The victim of a crime telling his or her story to the police may well be doing this: the words coming out vividly recall the experience, making them relive its pain, and the hand-over-mouth is an attempt to keep the words back in.

If you are telling a story to someone and they place hand or fingers over their mouth – it could mean they don't believe a word you're saying. Because it's where words come from, and primarily as humans we think we express ourselves through words, when we have any doubt or uncertainty about words our hands will go to our mouths.

There's an old story that has been recounted in various forms down the ages and in numerous countries. A rich man has a cache of precious jewels or gold in his house, but you don't know where. What do you do? Go into his house and shout 'Fire!' The man will instinctively run to where his treasure is hidden. In moments of crisis, we all run to what is most of value. When we think words are not doing what they should, our instinct is to stop them at source: the mouth.

A gesture many people tend to make is the old clapping-hand-over-mouth after saying something you shouldn't. It is often used now ironically or humorously; in other words, you really meant to let the cat out of the bag but joke that you didn't. Again, the gesture hints at pushing the words back in the mouth, forbidding their escape, even if it is too late.

Placing objects or fingers in the mouth. Babies who cry are offered dummies to suck as a substitute for their mother's breast. Small children who experience insecurity (even if it's only a temporary feeling of 'lostness') stick their thumbs in their mouths: again, the comfort this affords is intimately connected with memories of the security and nourishment of a mother's nipple.

Head, face and neck language

Adults, too, need their reassurance. The intimate link between mouth–comfort–nourishment has been put forward as an explanation for comfort eating, whereby some people under stress find a transitory comfort in consuming vast quantities of food, and even cigarette smoking; comfort is initially achieved by the repeated act of placing an object in the mouth, a comfort that all-too-rapidly transforms into an addiction to nicotine.

Indeed, smoking is thought by many to be a display of body language that signifies that a person is going though some kind of inner turmoil and is little to do with nicotine addiction at all. It is therefore considered but many in the field of psychology to be a classic displacement signal – that is, something that is substituted for something else. The reasoning behind this is that so many people are caught up in high-pressured jobs and instead of examining their lifestyles, they use a displacement activity such as smoking to release the tension that builds up on a day-to-day basis as a result of a stressful working and often personal life. Consider, for example, the tension that many of use feel when waiting to hear about exam results. Consider the scene outside an examination room. You can guarantee that there will be dozens of people outside puffing away, trying to alleviate the often intolerable amount of stress that a situation like an exam can bring. Other people who are non-smokers will probably be seen tapping their feet, pacing up and down or biting their nails. Thus smoking can be considered a part of body language that signifies anxiety and stress just as biting the nails and grinding the teeth can. These are all gestures that tell us that the person who is exhibiting this behaviour is in need of some relaxation.

The way in which a person smokes can also be seen to reflect their state of mind. Someone who smokes roll-up cigarettes for example, may find some kind of reassurance in the ritual involved in rolling a cigarette and the paraphernalia that they may use. The rolling if a cigarette requires many small, repetitive gestures that indicate that the person may be suffering from tensions. The way in which a person actually smokes a cigarette is also considered by many to be a reflection of their character or state of mind. One such aspect of a person smoking is the direction in which they are seen to blow their smoke. If people are feeling more positive, superior or confident than average, then they are likely to blow the smoke in an upward direction most of the time. In contrast to this, if people are feeling negative, dejected or lacking in confidence then they will tend to exhale the smoke in a downward direction most of the time. If they blow the smoke from the corner of their mouth, they are said to feeling exceptionally negative. This theory does not take into the fact that

Head, face and neck language

the smoker could be exhaling smoke in a direction that is less likely to annoy the person he is talking to, Such consideration is all the more likely in our current society which is becoming increasingly intolerant towards smoking.

Less extreme is the way in which children and adults place fingers and objects such as pencils or pens in the mouth for a good old chew.

The nose

Touching or covering the nose has been associated, as with mouth-covering, with deceit. Personally, I disagree. I think nose-touching or in some cases stroking the nose is an evaluative process. We all know the phrase 'I smell a rat'. People who touch or stroke their noses are wondering whether they do in fact smell a rat – whether what they're hearing or seeing is true; in stroking down the nose they're trying to tease out 'the smell' of a particular situation. The nose, after all, harbours our sense of smell, and that sense evaluates for us whether food is fresh or rotten, whether the air is clean or foul, whether something is clean or dirty.

Tapping the end of the nose is a decision-making trait. Some people cup their chin in their thumb and hold or tap the end of their nose at the same time – the classic pose of the thinker.

However, going back to my comments above about insecurity. Women who touch or cover their nose while speaking may in fact be doing so because they have a complex about the shape or size of their nose, and unconsciously they are trying to disguise it.

Head, face and neck language

The eyes

Just as we cover our ears in order not to hear, touching or rubbing the eyes signifies a desire not to see what we're seeing, or not to believe it. People who are describing difficult or emotional situations often, in fact, close their eyes, as if trying not to see what exists.

When people have to break bad news to other people, they can often close their eyes while telling them, or at least look down or away. It is a way of avoiding the pain of the situation.

The ears

To complete the hand-eye-mouth trilogy, covering the ears means we don't want to hear what it is we're hearing.

A finger placed inside the ear, even wiggled about as if cleaning the ear, means: 'I've had enough!' It's as if your words, or what you have been telling this person, are wriggling about in their ears like worms and they simply want rid of them. If someone does this while you are speaking to them, consider your options.

Head, face and neck language

The neck

Neck scratch. This is associated with doubt. If you tell someone an absolute porky, or present them with statistics or figures you know to be wildly inaccurate, and they scratch their neck – you're rumbled.

Collar/cuff pull. A nervous tugging at the collar and/or the cuff during speech have been associated with people who are not telling the truth. If lying causes heightened perspiration, then tugging at the collar and cuffs loosens the restriction of clothing and allows the sweat to pour more freely!

It is also a gesture associated with frustration, as if the person tugging at his collar or cuffs is literally trying to breathe, to free himself from restrictions. The Prince of Wales has been observed to tug his cuffs while speaking to the extent that impressionists 'doing him' are almost bound to copy this mannerism.

CHAPTER 13
The body language of sex

Perhaps the most prevalent use of body language occurs when we are flirting and trying to attract a potential partner. Certainly, as people tend to fear rejection when chatting someone up, it is often safer as well as being more seductive if we show someone that we like them by our body language rather than just coming out and saying it. This also avoids the danger of scaring someone off by being too direct or aggressive.

Flirting can be seen to induce certain physical changes in both sexes. For example, in both men and women research has shown that when flirting, their muscle tone is increased thus making them look younger and fitter, the bags under their eyes become less conspicuous making them look younger and more refreshed, their chest expands and the stomach is drawn in to make them appear slimmer.

In earlier sections, attention has been drawn to the

fact that body language may have different meanings when it is performed by people sexually attracted to one another as opposed to 'civilians'.

Studies have been done to show that when a woman approaches a group of men, it tends to bring out instinctive responses, such as patting down their hat or subconsciously straightening their ties. A highly aggressive sexual signal that men have been shown to make is when they assume the stance of a cowboy. This is when he can be seen to hook his thumbs under his belt turning his body towards the woman and pushing one foot forward whilst maintaining intense body language. We can only assume that all those westerns where the hero rides off into the sunset with the heroine have entered the popular consciousness somehow. A further stance that can be interpreted as sexually aggressive is for the man to stand with his hands on his hips or spreading his legs slightly. These positions are said to demonstrate a readiness for action.

A sign that a woman is attracted to the man she is talking to is when she is seen to toss her head, shaking out her hair. Although this probably began as a way of flicking the hair out of the eyes, the way that it shows off the colour and condition of the hair, a powerful tool of sexual attraction, meant that this gesture was used as a come-on signal. It has been observed that in modern times, when women are

The body language of sex

increasingly likely to have short hair that this gesture is just as common.

Another sign that both men and women are interested in the person they are talking to is if they show them their wrist or the palm of their hand. This is perhaps why smoking was originally considered sexy as it gives the person an excuse to show off their hand area and is perhaps why the dangerous femme fatale is never without a cigarette in film noir. Smoking has lost a great deal of this sexual appeal now that we are aware of the diseases it can cause as well as the damage it can do to our looks.

The postures generally assumed by men to indicate a sexual interest in the person that they are talking to are usually standing and this may be because masculinity is traditionally associated with dominance. However, if a woman wishes to indicate a sexual attraction to someone, she can often be seen to do so from a seated position. A common position adopted by a woman whilst speaking to someone whom she finds attractive is to sit with one leg folded underneath her so that the knee points towards the person that she is attracted to. Another gesture which can indicate that a woman is attracted to someone is if she slides her foot in and out of her shoe whilst talking to them. This allows her to show the delicate skin on the inside of her ankle and upper foot. On a more crude level, it can also be seen to mimic sexual intercourse. As far as heterosexual flirting goes, this gesture is said to be extremely provocative to men. It can also be alluring to a man if a woman crosses and uncrosses her legs with exaggerated slowness.

We have previously looked at the presence of both conscious and unconscious body language when we interact with others. The unconscious side of body language becomes all the more apparent when we flirt with someone. Our attempts to flirt are often more apparent to other than they are to ourselves. We may feel that we are being very subtle with regard to showing our attraction towards someone but our bodies tend to give us away. We may be completely unaware that whilst we say one thing with our mouths, we say something completely different with our bodies.

Most of the forms of body language that we have looked at can be applied to flirting to, such as the signals that someone is particularly nervous or enthusiastic. Just as eyes are an important medium through which body language becomes apparent, they are also invaluable when sending signals to a prospective partner. It is amazing how expressive the eyes can be and flirting is often little more that casting looks and glances which are loaded with meaning at the person whom we wish to attract and then waiting for his or her response.

When we look at someone that we are sexually

The body language of sex

attracted to, studies have been done to show that the tear glands start working harder and the eyes become slightly glazed in appearance. The pupils can also be seen to become dilated as though we are trying to see more of the person that we are looking at. Eyes are glazed with dilated pupils have been shown to be more attractive to other people, as though they are picking up these signals unconsciously.

When making eye contact, we should try and make effort not to blink too much. Blinking excessively can be interpreted as a sign of shyness or a lack of self-confidence and this can be unattractive to other people. If you wish to appear sincere and interested in a person then it is a good idea to maintain eye contact for a little longer than you would normally. This should not be too hard to convey as long as it is genuine. Remember – the eyes tend to convey our true feelings more than any other body part and can be guaranteed to give us away if we attempt to lie.

It is said to be particularly exciting for a man if a woman looks at him through lowered lids. Perhaps this is why Marilyn Monroe was often seen to lower her eyelids and peer through her eyelashes in publicity shots.

It is considered unattractive if a man looks about him when talking and cannot maintain eye contact. This is almost as if to say that he is so much of a

Casanova that he cannot stop looking out for other women even whilst he is in the middle of a conversation with one. It is also insulting for a woman to feel that her conversation is not fascinating enough to keep his attention as this keeps wandering off elsewhere. To impress a woman and to show her that you are interested in her, try and maintain eye contact. If she feels as though you cannot break your gaze away from her eyes, this will make her feel as though she is highly attractive to you.

If looking into the eyes of another person makes you feel a bit nervous or self-conscious, then it can be a good idea to look, instead, at the small space in between their eyes. Thus you are not making direct eye contact with them but to them it will appear as if you are. Another way of using the eyes is to wink at a prospective partner. However, this is sometimes seen as being a little crass and outdated and tends to only be used in an ironic way nowadays.

The mouth, which is another body part in expressing body language, is particularly expressive when flirting. We have already looked at how sensual the mouth is and how it is often considered to symbolise a woman's genitals. This erotic charge that the lips convey is heightened when a woman applies bright lipstick which mimics the way in which the lips and labia fill with blood during sexual arousal. It can also be highly seductive to apply lipstick in front

The body language of sex

of the person that you wish to attract. The act of applying lipstick can be very graceful, and when applying lipstick it is necessary to form a pout with the lips – another gesture which is said to be very appealing to men.

Other ways in which to use the mouth to appear sexually provocative is to part the lips slightly when looking at someone, lick or chew the lips, show the tongue without actually sticking it out or run the tongue along your teeth. These gestures should all be done with subtlety and a minimum of saliva or they can end up being more off-putting than alluring.

It can also be invaluable to look at and consider the meaning of the gestures that the object of your interest can be seen to display. For example, this can be his posture or his eye contact or lack of it. Remember that although his body language may be entirely unconscious, it should still give you vital clues as to what he thinks of you and whether there is a possibility of him returning your affections.

More than in any other sphere of life, it is in the realm of close intimate relationships that body language is used more than verbal language. As stated in the introduction, research has suggested that up to 65 per cent of our communication with each other is non-verbal; between two people in a sexual relationship, as much as 80 per cent of their communication with each other will be non-verbal.

After all, when two people are attracted to one another their aim will usually be to engage in the ultimate non-verbal piece of body language, the sexual act itself.

There is even a sub-text to the words we do use: it is as if being in love or in lust endows quite banal words with a deeper meaning, so it's possible, because of the tone of voice used, that a phrase like 'Please pass the sugar' can sound positively erotic. The voice is a subtle instrument, and as with any instrument different types of music can be played upon it. You have only to think of Marilyn Monroe in her sexier roles, or Sean Connery in the early Bond films, to understand how actors can use their voices (and quite ordinary dialogue) to convey sexuality.

When two people who are attracted to one another first meet, it is also a fact that they seldom listen to the words the other is using: the actual words are irrelevant. What the two are doing is reading each other's bodies, studying their eyes, faces, hands, legs, and the signals and messages these body parts are sending them. There's a very funny scene in an early Woody Allen film in which two people are sizing each other up as potential sexual partners. They are having a discussion about art: but flashed on the screen are sub-titles revealing what they are really thinking. Thus, the Diane Keaton character may be saying 'I thought that exhibition was really brilliant'

The body language of sex

but sub-titles show she's thinking 'Is my hair all right? I hope he likes long hair. Maybe he hates long hair and glasses!' In life, the woman would probably then touch her hair, or run her fingers through it, or toss her head – all ways of drawing attention to her hair, perhaps inviting the man to come back with 'You've got really lovely hair'.

Through countless TV documentaries, we're familiar with courtship rituals in the animal kingdom. Apart from survival -– finding food and escaping predators – the focus of an animal's life in the wild is the finding of a mate and the continuation of the species. Nature takes no chances with this; all species have an elaborate range of rituals, from grooming and preening to the outright display of some birds, designed to attract the attention and interest of a possible mate.

Human beings may have evolved a sophisticated and complex society, but when it comes to finding a mate, we are animals once again; it's even said that women who are ovulating have a different smell, which men detect subliminally and are unconsciously attracted by, knowing that this woman is 'ripe for breeding' and thus fulfilling her biological destiny. Some 'display' rituals tend to involve objects, for instance the importance to most men of the make and year of car they drive. Even in primitive societies, possessions have always conferred status (and, therefore, sexual allure) and his car is Western man's most prized possession. Look at the hours many of them spend cleaning (that is, 'grooming') their cars, in direct relation to the hours animals spend grooming themselves and others as part of their courtship rituals.

When we are attracted to another person, we automatically seem to care more about our appearance. If a colleague of yours suddenly seems to lose weight, acquire new clothes, have a change of hairstyle and (if female) wear more and different make-up, it's highly probable that she's 'met someone'. If you watch someone waiting for their date to turn up, you will see a great deal of fidgeting -- checking hair, adjusting collar and cuffs, flicking open the pocket make-up mirror – all of which is reassurance that they look OK. People newly in love are obsessed with mirrors, and can seldom pass one by without checking themselves.

We are highly sexualised creatures – according to Freud, even as babies we experience orgasm – and although centuries of established religion and societal rules have done their best to stifle and channel that sexuality, it still exists.

Cultural differences

As has been stated throughout this book, it is important to acknowledge that different cultures interpret behaviour differently. In many northern European countries, for instance, children are brought up with few inhibitions about their own bodies or nudity. They simply do not see nudity as a big deal. Equally, people from Scandinavia tend, on the whole, to be more openly affectionate with other people and to regard kissing and touching as everyday occurrences. Women from such countries who go on holiday to Mediterranean countries such as Greece or Italy may well find themselves regarded as 'easy', in extreme cases as little better than prostitutes. This is because in those cultures nudity is still often regarding as shocking and displays of affection are rarely given outside the family or in public. Everything about a Swedish woman might be regarded by some Mediterranean or Arabic men as a come-on, whereas in fact she is behaving perfectly normally according to her culture.

Rejection signals

Before we look at body language denoting the green light, it's as well to look at some red light signals. Physical attraction is not always a two-way process, though when we are attracted to someone we must always hope it will be. A great number of men end up with slapped faces or kneed groins because they simply have not been paying attention to the body language of the woman they are pursuing (often this is because alcohol has blurred their sensitivity).

First of all, what signals have you picked up about this woman's general body language? If she is a relaxed, open individual, who makes good eye contact with people to whom she is speaking and frequently touches her listeners on the arm or shoulder, then don't assume that because she does these things with you that there is a particular interest there. Come-on signals go far beyond ordinary 'open' social interaction.

Second, respect personal space until invited otherwise. Always allow someone a physical escape route: if you crowd the object of your interest up against a bookcase or into a corner at a party, you are literally blocking them in and imposing your presence in a way that can be repelling. Until you're sure of the other person, always insist in restaurants that they have the seat which allows a quick exit!

The body language of sex

If you're sitting next to the object of your affections on a sofa, don't automatically put your hand on the back of the sofa behind her. You are saying 'This is mine', and she may not yet be ready for that. If, however, her head is tilting towards yours, or even if her head is leaning back towards the arm of the sofa, this -- together with the rest of her body language – may be a positive signal.

Lack of interest, if not absolute rejection, can be picked up by the eyes, followed by the rest of the body. Eyes that constantly flicker away around the room, or appear distant and 'glazed' with boredom, are not the eyes for you; similarly if you are talking to someone and their feet or even their whole body are leaning or pointing away from you, back off.

Is the person you're trying to chat up speaking at their normal level? Almost always, if we are sexually attracted to someone we tend to lower and modulate our voices when speaking; we're probably not even aware we're doing this. This is because love always seems like a great secret, and we lower our voices when being secretive; more importantly, if you speak quietly the other person has to lean forward to hear you, thus entering your personal space. (Of course, it may also be that the other person has a naturally low voice, perhaps through lack of self-esteem, but if you lean forward and they lean back – the message is 'no'.) Incidentally, this is why discos and clubs are the least sexy places on the planet: intense noise means that in order to speak to anyone else you have to (a) shout and (b) place your mouth against their ear. All of which leads to immensely crossed signals and a huge number of unwanted one-night stands. If you are really looking for a life partner, don't try any of those places!

It was often said that one of the reasons the late Jackie Kennedy Onassis exerted such a powerfully magnetic effect upon men was her very low, soft speaking voice; men had to lean close enough to hear. Of course, she was also a beautiful and intelligent woman; she was undoubtedly also clever enough not to lean back, secure in her own strength in using body language for her own advantage. This is not to say that people who do consciously use body language are wrong to do so, merely that if you do, be very clear about your objectives.

The body language of sex

Body mirroring

When two people are in harmony with each other, they often adopt the same body posture. This is now a technique in some kinds of psychotherapy, aimed at putting the counsellee at ease and showing that the counsellor is in tune with them and empathic to their needs. More often, however, this mirroring is unconscious: if you look at two friends having an animated conversation, they will often be standing or sitting in the same way (same legs crossed, same tilt of head, and so on). These postures also change at the same time. If you uncross your legs, soon afterwards your friend will do so too.

The same is true of people who find each other physically attractive. Therefore, if the person you're with is doing the opposite – that is, not mirroring your body posture – then the chances are they're looking for an escape route.

Obvious and subtle signs of interest. Look at any one of a number of Hollywood movies (usually from the 1950s) or Italian films of the same vintage and you will see examples of overtly sexual body language. These range from pouting to emphasise full and kissable lips to licking the lips (not only to emphasise their readiness for a kiss but because the lips are a metaphor for a woman's vulva) to the walk: an open, rolling walk, thus emphasising the hips.

Women in such films would also often run their fingers through their hand, exaggerate a widening of the eyes, have soft husky voices, and throw their shoulders back so that their breasts would automatically be thrust forward and noticed. Overtly done, such body language is derided as being that of a vamp; but in more subtle forms, you can see the same in every area of life today.

Would-be lovers will originally indicate interest with the eyes (being able to hold the other's gaze longer than is normal in interactions with other people). When lovers gaze at one another, it tends to be across the eyes and below the chin to other parts of the person's body. When they are being particularly intimate, they look at the triangular area between the eyes and the chest or breast and for distant gazing from the eye to the crotch. Men and women use this gaze to show interest in each other and if the object of their affections is interested in them then they should be seen to return the gaze. This is coupled with the way in which their bodies seem directed towards each other which is the exact opposite of the 'pointing away' gestures we've talked about earlier. From that point on, the aim is to 'accidentally' brush the naked skin of the other person – meaning first the hands, and then the face. If someone for whom you feel antipathy or dislike hands you an object, you will try to avoid touching their hand as they do so; if for

The body language of sex

instance you are handed a glass by someone you're attracted to, you will (often quite unconsciously) try to brush your hand against theirs. Would-be lovers want to send each other the message 'I like you touching me, it's OK, go on'.

A woman's skin is one of her most sensitive organs. This is not just to do with fashion, although as a result 'revealing' dresses that expose flesh on arms, back and cleavage are considered sexy. When talking to a woman who feels attracted to you, you may notice that she finds opportunities to touch her own body, clothed or not: for instance, hugging her arms, or stroking her cheek, or rubbing a hand up and down her arms. She is, in essence, acknowledging that you might do the same at the appropriate time.

Note, however, that some women might just be doing this more because they find themselves attractive. Women (or, equally, men) who are very conscious of their own attractiveness to men (or women) will often behave as if they are attracted to the person they're speaking to, but in fact their chief focus of interest is themselves. The real clue here may lie in the eyes, which never lie.

Because we Brits live in a cold climate, and for reasons of convenience most of our bodies are covered most of the time, the flesh left unclothed (face, neck, hands, wrists, sometimes the neck and shoulders) assume sexual importance. In Victorian times, when female clothing covered almost 100% of the female form, an exposed ankle could drive a man into a frenzy. In the twenty-first century, when celebrities routinely appear in the press in clothes, or a lack of them, that leave little to the imagination, the picture is a little more confusing. Reverting to animal type, however, the parts of a woman's body that are usually still most appealing to men (breasts and buttocks) have either to do with reproduction or with the animal world, in which the rear-entry sexual position (which would emphasise the buttocks) is still the most common.

To sum up, then, the body language of sexual behaviour is the same as any other kind, but heightened.

Chapter 14
Posture

Posture describes the way the whole body moves and holds itself when still. Unconsciously, we reveal our personalities by the way we do this. The body posture of a person is usually either open or closed. It is a sure signal that if someone is feeling uncomfortable talking to someone else, then their body will automatically assume a closed position. He will more than likely have his legs crossed, his arms crossed in front of his chest, may hug his body for protection or may even hold something like a bag or a folder in front of his body. This bag or folder as well as his various crossed limbs make him feel as though he is more protected somehow and this may ease his sense of vulnerability.

This closed body position is usually adopted when talking to someone either we do not like or trust or someone that we simply do not know very well. The more we get to know someone and the more we trust them, the more likely it is that we will assume an open body position with them. In other words, with people we are intimate with, we will assume an open posture. The next time you are at a family gathering, observe your relatives as they talk and see what kind of posture they assume. Now if there is a newcomer in the group, for example, the new partner of a sibling, then consider their body language and how it differs from the other people in the group.

While the posture of most people can vary according to what social context they find themselves in, we can deduce general personality traits by studying people's postures. We can deduce much about as person and his character by examining his body posture, as the way in which people carry themselves reveals much about their character and their outlook on life. For example, if someone is feeling low then this will be obvious by the way that they carry themselves and hold their shoulders. We will be able to see signs of their depression in their body posture, as their shoulders will be hunched and sagging and their head will be lowered, and they will also seem reluctant to make eye contact when talking to other people. Nervous, insecure or depressed people will tend to close themselves in, as if trying to make themselves smaller and more inconspicuous, by folding the arms across the body, hunching the shoulders and dropping the head. They tend to omit

Posture

a signal to the rest of the world that they are uninterested in their surroundings or anyone or anything in them.

This posture can be directly contrasted to a confident person who walks straight and looks about them and appears to be interested in the world that surrounds them. It is no surprise that the more open, alert and welcoming the personality a person has, the more their posture will reflect this. Their head will be held up, balanced on the neck, the shoulders back, the chest open, the arms swinging naturally to the side. Our body posture tends to reflect exactly how we feel even if we are of a more moderate personality type than an extremely depressed or confident person. The next time you are feeling a little bit down or tired out, try walking upright and looking around you. The extra verbal stimuli will help take your mind off of any problem that is troubling you and assuming the posture of a confident, happy person should make you feel more confident and happy.

It is important to pay attention to our postures and maintain an upright open on is possible. In doing this, we are communicating with this posture that we are interested in and respectful towards the person that we are talking to. In turning your body to face the person that you are communicating with it shows that you are in hearing what they are trying to tell you. On a more general level, you are presenting an attitude of friendliness and acceptance towards the other person and if you present someone with a positive attitude then the it is all the more likely that they will mirror this positive body language back towards you. In making this small adjustment to your posture you are presenting a far more positive attitude to the outside world and will thus seem like a far more appealing person to those around you.

Posture is never a fixed entity: we can all change our posture instantly, according to mood. Studies have shown that when in the presence of people to whom they are attracted, most folk with straighten and open their posture. A man cam, for instance, be shuffling down the street with head and shoulders bowed, but once he spots a person for whom he has a particular feeling the shoulders will go back and the head will come up.

Most people at weddings will tend to have a more open posture, reflecting the happiness of the occasion; not surprisingly at funerals most will bow their heads and hunch their shoulders to reflect grief and sorrow.

We can ourselves affect our attitude and personality by our posture. Many who have, for instance, studied yoga or the Alexander Technique, or even taken dance classes, will notice a knock-on effect: these techniques variously aim to give us better

Posture

posture, making us more expansive and free and relaxed in the way we use our bodies. It is common for a lighter, freer personality to result from this. It is difficult to be depressed or negative with your head raised and your shoulders easily held back.

It's a fact that many people's posture is adversely affected by their work or their circumstances. Sitting for 8 or 9 hours at a desk every day, or hunched before a computer screen, tends to close the body up. People whose work makes them lead physically restricted lives need to be careful to give themselves plenty of opportunities – through posture awareness, and through a class such as yoga or dance – for openness and expansion. Even a half-hour daily walk in the fresh air, head up and arms swinging lightly by the side, can help enormously. The posture of those whose work allows them to be active in the fresh air – sports teachers, farmers and professional soldiers, for example – tends to be more upright and freer; soldiers and police offers in particular are noted for their upright, even rigid, bearing.

We don't see ourselves asleep and few other people in our lives do, but the posture we typically adopt when lying down is also body language. Some people revert to the foetal position: that is, lying on the side, hugging the knees towards the chest and folding the arms around the body. Not surprisingly, such people are subconsciously seeking the safety and protection of their mother's womb; their reaction to the pressures of the world is to adopt that position of maximum security. The semi-foetal position is one of the most common sleeping postures. Here the knees are loosely and only slightly draw up, and the arms loosely held in front of the head: instead of suggesting a need for safety, this position actually indicates relaxation. A sleeping person is a vulnerable person, so it makes sense to protect ourselves to a certain extent, but this position suggests a restful night and allows the body to move frequently, as is natural during sleep.

By contrast, those who sleep on their backs, arms by their sides, suggest confidence and invulnerability: they obviously don't feel the need to protect themselves in any way. It's also, incidentally, a position more likely to lead to snoring!

People who lie face down, often with the arms stretched out or curled in a protective manner around the head are needing to protect themselves – it's the position adopted when a bomb goes off or a gun goes off, and suggests that the person perceives danger around them.

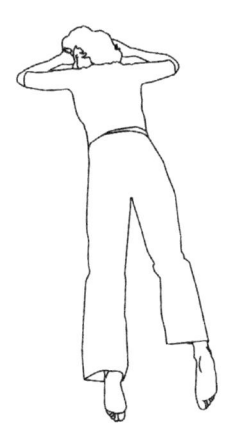

Chapter 15
Making body language work for you

The Interview

The previous chapters should have given you an idea of various ways in which your body can reflect your state of mind. While we have acknowledged the idea that it is not a good idea to consciously use body language to manipulate or trick people, there is nothing wrong in being aware of the signals that your body gives off and using this to your advantage. There are many situations where it is particularly useful to be aware of your body language and the message that is given out by this. For example, on a first date, or when meeting people for the first time, we are more likely to make an effort to project a particular part of our personality, whether this be in order to show a new acquaintance that we are a friendly approachable person or to show a boss that we are professional and capable in the context of the workplace.

In previous chapters we have explored the idea that body language is generally unconscious and alters the way other people perceive us. It is important to be aware of how much our body language does determine the impression that we give to other people. Often people with a low sense of self worth convince themselves that they are in some way ugly or unattractive. This can then be a self-fulfilling prophecy as they adopt the body language of someone who believes themselves to be worthless or unattractive and give this message to others. In social interaction, this erroneous belief is then confirmed as other people are unlikely to befriend or want to form relationships with someone whose body language tells them that they are not worth getting to know.

It is clear that through our body language, we tell other people how we expect to be treated. When someone with low self esteem first meets another person, they are likely to start having thoughts like, "They are not going to like me. Even if they seem to like me at first, someone will tell them not to or they will find out what I'm really like and go off me. This person, so lacking in confidence, will tend to avoid eye contact as much as possible. They will stand with shoulders curved in as if trying to make themselves as small and inconspicuous as possible. They may mumble as if what they are trying to say is not worth

Making body language work for you

listening to. They may even be seen to criticise a mutual acquaintance in order to take the attention off of themselves and direct it elsewhere. These reactions combine to create very negative body language and this cannot help but influence how that person is perceived. Most of us have been in a situation where we have met someone who appears to be very attractive, but when they begin talking they are so negative that it detracts from how attractive they are. Most people respond to open, friendly people who seem positive about themselves and about life in general.

A situation in which most people would admit to being more conscious of their body language and the message that it conveys to other is that of the interview. While we all use body language to project our personalities during the interview, if not modified or controlled, body language can be a double-edged sword and can detract from our performance more easily than it can enhance the favourable impression that we are trying to make on the interviewer. In an interview situation, most of us would admit to being a little more nervous than usual and often this can spark off clusters of physical reactions that combine to produce signals that we are ill at ease and uncomfortable with the situation. With a little analysis, work and practise, it is possible to modify our behaviour in situations like interviews, ensuring that we are able not only to cope with such a potentially stressful situations but also able to conquer these feelings of nervousness and instead give off the impression that we are in fact comfortable and in control.

Often being able to give an impression of a particular state of mind, actually allows us to feel this state of mind in reality. In other words, if we are able to appear calm and relaxed we are far more likely to start to feel calm and relaxed. This is one of the reasons that we are often told to take deep breaths and consciously attempt to relax our muscles when we are feeling nervous. It is thought that if we can make our body relax in this way then our mind will follow and also become more relaxed. The same holds true for body language. If we give off signals of being calm and relaxed, whether consciously or unconsciously, it is highly likely that we will begin to feel these emotions. Thus is the power of the mind and positive thought. We will now consider the interview situation as well as looking at ways in which you can make your body language work for you instead of against you and combine to create a positive and favourable impression on any future employer.

So, if body language can be defined as small physical reactions which combine to give off signals which reflect our state of mind, then it follows that

Making body language work for you

we can be aware of the reactions that we are likely to display when experiencing a particular emotion and then try to counteract any negative reactions and replace them with more positive ones. Here is a quick recap of some typical examples of how body language can be interpreted.

Of course we wish to appear confident during an interview and we can become so caught up in feelings of nervousness that it is easy to forget that a few simple behaviours can make all the difference to the impression that we give off and in turn how we are perceived by the interviewer. When we first enter the room and indeed for the duration of the interview, it is very important that we make an effort to smile. Smiling can make a huge difference to the initial impression that we give to our interviewer and it is a truism that initial impressions are longer-lasting than any other and very difficult to change at a later date. A large, open-lipped smile is a small action but can say more than 1,000 words and the most impressive CV put together. Such a smile only takes a second, but it says that we are a happy, confident and relaxed person with a positive attitude towards life and towards other people. It expresses enthusiasm which most employers would say is a must for the position that they are advertising. A wide smile also gives the impression that the person is entirely open and honest and has nothing to hide. This is essential especially when applying for a position where trustworthiness is a particularly important quality. Smiling also indicates a friendly person who is friendly and approachable and is easy to get on with. Many employers realise the importance of an employee displaying these attributes, particularly nowadays when the values of team work and co-operation are so highly esteemed.

Other ways to display that you are a friendly, open and warm person include sitting with your hands on your lap, leaving the palms open and visible to the interviewer. Again this shows that you are relaxed, happy and have nothing to hide from him or her. It is also a good idea to unbutton your coat upon sitting down. This will prevent you from overheating which is easy to do when you are nervous and becoming uncomfortable during the interview. From a body language point of view, it again gives the impression that you are an open and relaxed person who is comfortable with any situation that you may find yourself in. These qualities are considered invaluable for most positions you could be applying for.

Signals that we are feeling particularly confident in a situation are if we stand tall and walk into the room with our shoulders back and our chins up high and proceed to make direct eye-contact with whoever is in the room. In fact one way to give away the fact that you may be feeling less than confident is if you avoid the eye-contact of others. This can be interpreted in an even more negative way as being a sign of shiftiness or untrustworthiness; the fact that you cannot look people in the eye suggests that you have something to hide from them. Further examples of body language that indicate that we are feeling confident are if we either sit up straight or even lean forward in the chair. Leaning forward suggests an eagerness to communicate with and get to know the interviewer. In contrast, slouching or sliding down in the chair indicates that we are trying to make ourselves smaller or more invisible and escape the penetrating gaze of the interviewer. Other signals of confidence are if we are seen to place the tips of the fingers of one hand against those of the other hand in a praying or "steeple" position. To do this requires that we have steady hands, thus it reflects a calm, confident demeanour. It is also a sign of confidence if we are seen to join the hands together behind the back when standing. Again, this shows that we are an open and friendly person with nothing to hide. It also reflects a relaxed state of mind as it shows that we are so comfortable with the person that we are talking to that we do not need to cover our body in any way by for example curling the shoulders, hugging ourselves or sitting with our arms crossed in what can be perceived as a defensive stance.

There are also a variety of signals that we are

feeling less than confident or even downright terrified in an interview situation. If we are given the option of smoking it is usually a good idea to decline – even if the interviewer is seen to have a cigarette.

Smoking is often considered a sign of nervousness and furthermore it can be seen as a sign of discipline and self control if we admit to being a smoker but show that we do not need to smoke even in as stressful a situation as an interview. Another sign of nervousness is whistling. While we are highly unlikely to start whistling in the middle of an interview, it is worth remembering that it can convey a sense of nervousness. Other signs of nervousness include pinching the skin, rubbing arms or fiddling with hair, scratching, jingling the contents of our pockets, running your tongue over your teeth, twisting fingers together, picking at the hem of your clothes, twiddling your thumbs or clicking the tongue. Biting your nails is another classic sign of nervousness and even if you do not bite your nails in the actual interview, most interviewers are trained to be observant enough to notice if your nails have been bitten down to the quick. It is therefore a good idea to try and refrain from biting your nails in the run-up to the interview so that this small but significant sign does not give you away. If Willpower alone is not enough to make you stop then it may be worth investing in one of the special deterrents that come in

Making body language work for you

the form of a nail polish or even book yourself in for a few sessions of hypnotherapy.

Indeed, anything that can be considered a fidgeting action can be interpreted as a sign of nervousness. If you are in this situation and find that you have the urge to start biting your nails or drumming your fingers, then it is a good idea to try and relax, breathe deeply and concentrate all your attention on what the interviewer is actually asking you. Often we are so nervous that we do not pay close attention to what is being said. Then when we are actually asked a question, we find that we have no idea how to respond. This in turn makes us more nervous and less able to piece together some sort of respectable answer which makes us more nervous and more likely to display nervous body language. This vicious circle is very difficult, but not impossible to break.

There are other signs of nervousness that our bodies can display that are less easy to disguise. For example when nervous we may start to sweat more, become flushed, our voices can seem unnaturally high and we can speak more quickly than usual and lose the train of our thoughts far more easily. As these are more involuntary than other forms of body language, they are much harder to counteract. It is therefore a good idea just to concentrate on relaxing in general and on inhibiting those behaviours which are easy to control and hopefully these involuntary responses will start to disappear automatically.

It is not just nervousness that must be counteracted during an interview. Another form of negative behaviour is to show through body language that you are untrustworthy or defensive. These two traits are often indicated by very similar sets of body language. Examples of types of body language that combine to show that we are untrustworthy or defensive are if we are seen to frown excessively, squint our eyes, smile but in a fixed or tense manner, cross our arms as if we are trying to protect our body, pull away quickly when shaking someone's hand or have our chin pointing downwards as though as are trying to make ourselves less conspicuous. Other signs of trustworthiness include avoiding eye contact when speaking as though we have something to hide, rub the back of our neck, touching our face as though we are extra conscious of the area of ourselves that the interviewer is focussing on and darting our eyes about again to avoid prolonged eye contact. Gesturing with our hands clenched into a fist, hitting them off one another or pointing with an extended index finger are all movements that indicate excess aggression or tension. Clasping the hands behind the whilst leaning back in the chair is also seen to indicate that we are not entirely comfortable as can be seen to show that the person is attempting to feign

Making body language work for you

being comfortable and relaxed but this looks too contrived.

It is clear from the examples that we have looked at that there are many types of body language that can give the interviewer a window on our state of mind during an interview. It is also apparent that there are far more negative than positive signals and there are probably many more than we are even consciously aware of. The above examples are simply the more obvious forms of body language but tiny movements and inflections can also be hugely suggestive when they combine to form larger clusters of body language.

It is not a good idea to study the examples of body language that give off the impression of confidence and then attempt to display every single one of these examples in an interview. The strain of attempting to behave in a way that was entirely unnatural would only serve to increase your nervousness and it could backfire. Moreover, most interviewers are experienced enough to see through interviewees attempts to appear more confident, intelligent or interesting than they actually are and will not be impressed if they sense that you are somehow trying to pull the wool over their eyes and deceive them as to your true character. We have studied these examples of positive and negative examples of body language not so the positive ones can be artificially adopted, but we are aware of and therefore can avoid the more negative types of behaviour. If you have a habit of doing any of the above negative examples, try to train yourself to avoid this pattern of behaviour by remembering each time you feel yourself starting to do it what negative signal it could be sending out to other people. If you practice training yourself to avoid this now then you will be less likely to display any such behaviour in the interview without having to make a huge effort to remember not to. This will allow you in turn to concentrate more on listening to questions and formulating sensible, relevant and coherent answers. It is also a good idea not only to monitor your own body language but also that of the person who is conducting the interview. Throughout the course of the interview, try and develop an awareness of their body language and non-verbal cues. Do not concentrate on this to the extent of neglecting your own performance and do not try to read in more than is actually being communicated as this can be counterproductive and can make your own responses seem erratic and inconsistent if you keep changing tack in response to what you imagine are the interviewers unconscious responses. It is possible to develop a sense of the interviewer's perception of you. The most obvious example that you have achieved a positive connection with the interviewer is if

Making body language work for you

whenever you smile, the interviewer in turn responds with a smile. Also, this should be an open, relaxed smile which involves the eyes as well as the mouth. If this smile seems at all strained or forced then it could be that the interviewer is being patronising or is trying to disguise his or her dislike or disapproval of you. Another obvious signal is if the interviewer's eyes start to wander, they stifle a yawn, or their eyes glaze over when you are speaking, then it is probably safe to assume that you have given a sufficiently long answer to the question and it is time to stop talking and allow your interviewer to move on to their next question. Try to stay conscious of your interviewer's reactions - both verbal and non-verbal ones –and this will give you some guidance as to how the interview is proceeding and may even give you some reassurance and increased confidence that the interview is going well.

Group Activities

If you want to examine your body language in greater depth or look at ways of improving the impression that you create on other people then it is possible to carry out exercises with this in mind. You can do this alone but it is often more rewarding and productive to do it with other people. You can check in your local library or community centre to see if there is some kind of class already in existence that you could join. If there is not, then why not team up with some likeminded people and start your own? Obviously the more people that become involved, there more input there will be and the more effective these exercises will be, but if you cannot find enough people to form a group then it is worth asking friends or partners if they are prepared to become involved.

Here are some examples of exercises that you can do to hone your ability both to detect the subtle behaviour that you display which can distort peoples' perception of you and to allow you to suppress any behaviour that is giving out negative signals. These exercises are fun to do and are also useful if you have an interest in drama or the performing arts.

Making body language work for you

Exercise 1
Studying hand gestures

One way of learning more about body language is to get into pairs and perform various role plays. The members of the group that are not participating can them observe a particular aspect of body language as well the context that this was displayed in. One aspect of body language that has many different forms and can mean many things in different contexts is any gesture which is made by the hands. Ask each pair in the group to act out a role play where they have to pretend to be nervous or angry or exasperated and ask the remainder of the group to pick out hand gestures which exemplify these emotions, collecting the various examples on a black board. Members of the group will no doubt be surprised at gestures that they have been seen to display and it is possible to collect many different types of hand gesture. It is also useful to consider how these hand gestures combine with other gestures of, for example, the face and other body movements to convey a general emotion or state of mind. Consider as well how these hand gestures can vary in meaning from culture to culture – a topic we have touched upon in various chapters. Different members of the group will probably be able to contribute various examples of this that they have read about or encountered in travels abroad.

Exercise 2
Exploring body language in various contexts

While the first exercise explores how body language changes to reflect the emotion of the person who is exhibiting it, it is also common for the same person to display very different body language depending on the location that they find themselves in. One place where there can be said to be a code of behaviour which is inevitably reflected in the body language of people is in a public bar. A bar can be considered a microcosm of the real world where a small but cross section of society find themselves in the same place at the same time. Bars are also considered by many to be a place where it is more acceptable to approach a stranger to make conversation with the intention of meeting someone with whom one could possible become romantically involved. That is why more downmarket bars are often referred to as "meat markets".

A useful exercise particularly for those people in the group who wish to meet a romantic partner is to discuss the body language that can often be seen in a bar or club. Consider what personality types you may meet in a bar and how their body language can contribute to the impression that we have of their personalities. Ask each member of the group to recount a situation where they have felt

Making body language work for you

uncomfortable or angry at the body language of someone else in the pub. This could include an example of lecherous behaviour or could be a time when they have felt threatened by the overpowering or aggressive behaviour of another person. You should consider various aspects of body language such as the amount of space that you are given by the person that you are interacting with, the posture of that person, the presence or absence of eye contact and any other form of body language we have considered already.

It can be interesting for members of the group to consider those examples of body language that they find pleasing when they speak to someone else. For example most people are bound to say that they prefer someone who smiles when they first meet, but there are likely to be less obvious examples of body language that not everyone has previously been aware of.

Exercise 3
Mirroring Each Other's Body Language

This is a common exercise used in drama classes for aspiring method actors, and it an interesting way to highlight forms of behaviour by having another person pick out the most apparent and reflect them like a mirror image. Again, the group should all pair off, then one person in each pair becomes the leader and the other, the follower.

The leader should then start displaying various signs of body language and he follower must copy these. The person who is leading should attempt to use a wide range of body language to show examples of many different emotions or states of mind. The couple should then swap roles with the person who previously followed becoming the leader. The pair should practise this for a minute or two and then attempt to mirror each others body language with neither person leading.

This exercise can be done using mainly facial expressions or hand gestures – whatever the leader decides. There is no limit to the types of body language used and this exercise is an invaluable way of examining body language in greater detail. It is also interesting to note the similarities and differences between each person and the types of body language that they choose when leading. The final exercise

Making body language work for you

where no-one in particular is selected to lead can show a difference in character between the two people as often a natural leader emerges. The more balanced the two characters, the more successful this final exercise will be.

Exercise 4
Non-Scripted Role Plays

For this exercise, the group can be divided into twos and threes, depending on how many people are in the group. You should then ask each group to invent a role play where the characters communicate through body language alone and use no form of verbal communication. Each group has free reign over the nature of the role play and the type of characters that they will pretend to be. This exercise is more effective if the role play is not planned ahead too much and is more or less made up as it happens. A way of doing this is to set the scene, loosely sketch the characters that will be in the scene and think of a few possible plots that the scene many involve. Then go ahead and improvise a scene around this vague plan. This allows each group to be more relaxed and spontaneous and therefore more inclined to display natural and unforced examples of body language.

Each of the smaller groups should then perform their role plays in front of the rest of the group. If they wish, the smaller groups can set the initial scene of the role play by saying where it is and who the characters are but after this initial introduction the communication should be entirely non-verbal. It is also possible to carry out the role plays without introducing them so that the groups have to rely

Making body language work for you

entirely up on body language for communication

Ideas for possible role plays to act out are:

- You have turned up on a blind date only to discover that you have been set up with someone from your work that you do not get on with.

- You have had a fight with your partner but are having dinner with friends and have to pretend to not be angry with each other.

- You are going away on holiday and arrive at the airport only to discover that your baggage has been lost.

Use any of these examples or alternatively, make up some of your own. Any situation that involves conflicting emotions or a range of emotions makes the basis for an interesting role play. Each group should perform its improvisation in front of the others while the other should study the various examples of body language on display and the emotions that they are conveying. After each role play, the class discusses what they believe was happening in the scene based on what they saw in the body language. What are the personalities of the people involved? What are their relationships to each other? Are these relationships happy or strained? What are the main issues that influence the people in the group? This exercise should serve as an effective springboard for starting an in-depth discussion about the various types of body language and how they can be interpreted.

Chapter 16
Body language in the workplace

We have just looked at how the phenomenon of body language can both help and hinder us during a situation like an interview where it is imperative that we make a positive first impression. However, it is also important that once we are successful at an interview and chosen for a position that we continue to consider our body language once we start the job. We have already studied the area of space and territory in the workplace and what this tells us about people but it is also important to look at our individual body language when we interact with other people in the workplace and the impression that this makes on them. The study of body language is particularly beneficial in areas such as sales, as in order to sell something, we need to gain the trust and even the approval of the person that we are selling to. If someone does not get a good impression from a sales person, then they are unlikely to buy anything from them, no matter how attractive the product is. Although, particularly important for this kind of profession, a good general awareness of body language can be highly useful in most positions.

When dealing with clients in any area of work, it is much easier to establish a good working relationship if you are able to build up a sense of rapport with someone. This can be done through conveying that you are able to see things from their point of view and by establishing this sense of empathy. This can be done through a variety of ways, including the gestures and expressions of body language. We have already acknowledged the claim by researchers that it is our body language more than any other factor that creates the impression that we first make on other people. Thus, most communication is done without words – a phenomenon that many employers have been slow to pick up on and use for the good of their employers.

When we first meet a client or colleague, we have seconds in which to make a good impression. This impression will not be completely permanent and may change over time but once it is made it can prove hard to change. Since it is our body language that holds the most sway then it doesn't matter if we are an entertaining conversationalist or if we can impress a client by an expert knowledge of our line of work. It is imperative if we want to make a favourable

Body language in the workplace

impression that we are aware of the body language that we are displaying and what this says about our attitude towards our work as well as our sense of empathy with colleagues and clients and our personal ethics and values.

As society becomes increasingly centred around work with both men and women taking their careers more seriously than ever before, it is all the more important to consider the role that body language can have in business. Workplaces are also becoming more people-orientated and are more concerned with how people are treated by colleagues and bosses and with how content they are in their jobs. This more caring and humane approach to the workplace could be explained by the steep rise of successful women in the business world as women are traditionally associated with having a more caring approach to life. Aggressive attempts to further one's career at the expense of others such as bullying or old-boy networking are now treated as serious offences and companies are likely to be taken to tribunals for unfair treatment of their staff. It is therefore vital that staff are made to feel appreciated and shown respect and there is no better way to do this than through body language.

When meeting clients it is considered polite to shake their hand, so this can be considered a good place to start when considering the message that your body language gives to others in the workplace. In our chapter on gestures and gesticulation, we looked at various types of handshake and the messages that these can give off. A handshake can be too soft, too firm, too brief, too long, or even painful. The way you shake hands gives the other person an insight into your character. Aggressive people tend to have very firm handshakes. People with low self esteem are said to have a soft and often limp handshake. When people are trying to give a good impression, they often shake your hand with their other hand covering the shake or holding your elbow. This in itself can be seen as a sign that someone is untrustworthy, as it tends to be the favoured handshake of politicians. Many women report that the more chauvinist men in the workplace tend to crush women's hands, almost as if trying to crush them into submission. A good defence against this underhand tactic is to more your index and little finger in towards the palm. This makes it harder for someone else to crush whilst silently asserting yourself against a supposed act of aggression. It is usually considered most effective to adopt a handshake that is neither limp nor aggressively firm. This will convey an impression of you as a level-headed, professional who is neither too weak nor too aggressive. It is also a good idea to regularly wash your hands as cool dry hands are far more pleasant to the touch than warm moist hands.

Body language in the workplace

Posture is another example of body language that takes on particular importance in the workplace. We have already considered the notion that slouching and drawing the shoulders in can make someone look as if they are lacking in confidence, whilst standing straight and tall makes a person look happy, confident, open and most of all reliable. Being reliable and capable is one of the most important character traits in any workplace. If you want your boss to trust you enough to give you sole charge of a particular job or project then it is highly important that you give off an impression of being reliable. Also the more open you appear to be the more someone feels that they can trust you with a position of responsibility.

We have already considered the phenomenon of verbal highlighting – that is the tendency to preface speech with phrases such as, "To be honest…" or "To tell you the truth…" When people hear phrases such as these automatic alarms bells start to ring. If you are indeed being honest then there is no need to point this out. It will become apparent by your body language. The fact that someone has to insist that they are being honest often suggests that they are trying too hard and therefore may not be being entirely honest. Instead of telling someone to trust you, try simply to appear sincere and trustworthy. If you are a trustworthy person, then this should not be too difficult to put across to someone else.

When talking to a client remember, to instil them with a sense of trust by leaving your palms open and visible. Combine this with an open posture and sincere facial expression for maximum effect. As many people associate crossed arms with low self-esteem or an attempt to hide something then it is probably best to keep arms hanging by your sides. As we have previously acknowledged, the correct amount of eye contact will reassure the person you are speaking to that you are a trustworthy, approachable person. If your eyes are looking about all over the place, this tends to suggest that you are not speaking the truth and are too afraid to make contact lest your eyes give you away. Furthermore, when breaking eye contact for a second it is better to look to the left-hand side, as this is break eye contact and look to the right, the person you are speaking to may get the impression that you are being dishonest about something. Neither is it a good idea to look down when talking to someone as this is said to be a typical action of someone with low self-esteem and this will not be impressive to a prospective client or colleague. Colleagues are likely to be equally unimpressed if you wear sunglasses. Many people are tempted to use sunglasses as they think that they make them look stylish whilst giving the impression of a protective barrier between them and the rest of the world. However, someone who wears sunglasses when there

Body language in the workplace

is no glaring sun about to justify it can often be take for a bit of a poseur. Furthermore, sunglasses can suggest to the outside world that you have something to hide and are therefore not to be trusted.

When you are meeting a client for the first time it is important to use open gestures. To convey as sense of honesty. Enthusiasm is also an important quality to be seen to have in business. One way of conveying a sense of enthusiasm and positivity is to use outward and upward movements of your hands. An appropriate time to do this would perhaps be during a presentation when using a flipchart.

If you wish to advance your career, it is important to show that you are confident. This can be shown in many ways. A good way of showing confidence that we have previously looked at is to shape your fingers like a steeple. This is not only effective at displaying confidence. It also gives you something to do with your hands to take your mind off your nerves whilst also avoiding making fidgeting movements which may convey nerves. However, it is important to avoid looking over-confident or colleagues may feel that you are overbearing or aggressive and may avoid you. One examples of body language that can suggest cockiness is if you are seen to clasp your hands behind your head as you lean back in a chair.

A further useful pose to suggest eagerness and readiness to become involved with a project is if you stand with your hands on your hips. Another positive gesture when talking to a client or colleague is to unbutton your suit jacket in front of them. This shows that while you dress smartly, you do not feel that need to keep up an excessively formal front and are open and flexible in your approaches to work. If you take off your suit jacket entirely then you intensify the effect of this action. Going one stage further by rolling your sleeves up suggests that you are willing and ready to get stuck into work. Obviously, making these gestures should not be forced.

If a business meeting is not going particularly well then being all gung-ho may scare off potential clients all the more. Play it by ear according to each individual situation.

As you talk with a client, it is important to always be watching their body language. If they appear defensive by frowning or crossing their arms, then attempt to use positive signals and statements that will reassure them and allow them to relax. No matter how uncomfortable they seem, never stop appearing open and cheerful and hopefully this positive attitude will begin to rub off on them. If there is something that you wish to propose such as a new idea that you have for the business then wait until the body language of others is open and positive before you broach it. No matter how good your idea is, it will be

Body language in the workplace

harder to sell to others if they are predisposed to being hostile and suspicious. It is up to you and your body language to reassure them and prepare them to take on board new ideas. You will know when it is a good time to broach a proposition because their body language will start to appear more relaxed and open. If and when they begin to mirror your body movements, you will know that they are being very receptive towards you and then is the time to act. They are taking in your words and are responding to them well. We have already looked at mirroring in some detail. To quickly recap, mirroring is a phenomenon whereby, when two people are in tune with one another, one person imitates the body language other the other person and vice versa.

When giving a talk or trying to persuade a colleague to back a particular project or idea of yours, it is a good idea to use a technique known as "tracking". This is where you mirror their body language, and once they have become attuned to your mirroring of their body language, they are more likely to respond by mirroring yours. You should slowly display more and more open and positive body language and the person whom you are speaking to will become more reassured and should begin to display this body language too. The effect of displaying a certain cluster of body language is that it can slowly affect a person's frame of mind. This means that by displaying positive body language, a person should start to become more positive.

If, when you are talking to a colleague, they touch themselves about the face or cover their mouth, this is said to show that they are withdrawing from your company. This may be because you have done or said something that has made them feel uncomfortable. If this occurs, it may be a good idea to change tack with approach you were using. If you wish to convince someone of your sincerity then it can be a good idea to show your palms. We have already looked at the connection between displaying the palms and honesty in our chapter on gestures and gesticulation. Do not attempt to use body language to show that you are being honest if you are in fact trying to deceive someone. This is unethical and it is unlikely to be successful anyway as the eyes usually give us away when we try to lie.

Just as it is important to seem trustworthy to clients and colleagues it is also important to appear confident. If you fidget, you will appear nervous and lacking in self-esteem. This can be damaging enough to your social life, but in the workplace it can seriously affect your career. Colleagues will seriously doubt your ability to cope with work if you appear to be riddled with self-doubt. So remember, stand stall and make good steady eye contact. There is plenty more information on ways to appear confident

Body language in the workplace

throughout this book. While it is imperative that you appear confident, it is just as important that you do not appear too aggressive. If you are seen to be aggressive then people will sense that you are potentially competition to them and they will be less likely to co-operate with you. So avoid gestures such as leaning back with your hands behind your head and pointing in an aggressive manner at someone.

An awareness of body language in the workplace can be a very useful thing. For example, if you sense that a client is disgruntled about something you can calm them down with body language and then get to the root of the problem. Remember to always maintain an awareness of your body language and that of other people in the workplace. If you believe in your own capability and are honest and fair in your dealings with other people then this should come across in your body language. The rest may need a little fine-tuning but maintain an open and friendly attitude and you should be fine.

In conclusion...

This book has been no more than a brief introduction to the fascinating study of body language. It's worth just reminding ourselves of one or two of the main points again. First, gestures are individual movements of body parts, and many of these are consciously or deliberately made; body language, on the other hand, is a whole cluster of gestures or movements, most of which is quite unconscious. We may lie with words and with verbal communication, but not with the language of the body, which will always reveal our truest, deepest feelings. The more we understand what the body is saying about how we feel, the more we can address our negative feelings or insecurities, and acquire greater confidence and openness in our manner. And we should always study other people's body language in context, and never ignore the obvious. The man who is hugging himself at the bus-stop in the rain may not be deeply self-protective or insecure, he could just be wet and cold; while the woman at the party who keeps crossing and uncrossing her legs need not be sending out signals of sexual attraction for you, she could just be longing to go to the bathroom!

As in all psychological studies, maintain your humour and your sense of balance (literally as well as in terms of body language), and you won't go far wrong.